BRANDED MALE

BRANDED MALE

MARKETING TO MEN

Mark Tungate

KOGAN PAGE

London and Philadelphia

First published in Great Britain and the United States in 2008 by Kogan Page Limited.

120 Pentonville Road
London N1 9JN
United Kingdom
www.kogan-page.co.uk

525 South 4th Street, #241
Philadelphia PA 19147
USA

© Mark Tungate, 2008

The right of Mark Tungate to be identified as the author of this work has been asserted by him in accordance with the Copyright, Designs and Patents Act 1988.

ISBN 978 0 7494 5011 3

British Library Cataloguing-in-Publication Data

A CIP record for this book is available from the British Library.

Library of Congress Cataloging-in-Publication Data

Tungate, Mark, 1967–
    Branded male : marketing to men / Mark Tungate.
        p. cm.
    Include bibliographical references.
    ISBN 978-0-7494-5011-3
 1. Branding (Marketing) 2. Male consumers. 3. Target marketing. I. Title.
    HF5415.1255.T86 2008
    658.80081--dc22
                                                        2007047299

Typeset by JS Typesetting Ltd, Porthcawl, Mid Glamorgan
Printed and bound in Great Britain by MPG Books Ltd, Bodmin, Cornwall

For Tim – the original

Contents

Acknowledgements

Like most men, I enjoy a bit of bonding. And so I'd like to thank those who bonded with me during the course of this project. I am grateful to all my interviewees, of course – especially Margaret Jobling of Unilever, who partly inspired *Branded Male* and who, unknowingly, became its guardian angel, because I kept her in mind during the writing process. Mark Simpson, 'the father of metrosexuality', provided time above and beyond the call of duty; as did Genevieve Flaven of Style-Vision. I'd also like to thank Tony Quinn of Magforum, for tweaking the chapter about men's magazines. And I'm grateful to Alison Bishop of WGSN for her enthusiasm and advice. Thanks are long overdue to all at Kogan Page, particularly Jon and Martha – and especially Pauline Goodwin, who started me out on this adventure.

The other members of my crack team of man-hunters were: Ingrid Bal (Philips); Joanna Christie (Dunhill); Allison Clark (Match. com); Alpana Deshmukh (D&D London); Susannah Donnelly (*The Times*); Clare Fleerackers (Diageo); Sian Griffiths (Peninsula Hotels); Mark Harrison (BMW); Anoushka Healy (*The Times*); Katherine Highland (BMW); Inga Ruby (Gieves & Hawkes); Marian Webb (Hilton); and Vanessa Munnings (Myriad PR).

Finally, as ever, I'd like to thank Géraldine for her love and support. To paraphrase the late James Brown, this man's world would be 'nothing, without a woman or a girl'.

Introduction

This book began with a shirt. A blue cotton chambray shirt – a little better cut than most, but otherwise perfectly ordinary. When I tried it on, however, I found that the sleeves were too long. Before I could fold back the offending cuffs, the saleswoman was at my side. 'They're all like that now,' she told me. 'It's the motorcycle cut.' I looked slantwise at her: *the motorcycle cut*? She extended her arms. 'When you're on a motorbike you reach forward, like this, and the sleeves ride up. Guys tell us they like the sleeves cut a bit longer, so they look good when they're on their bikes.'

I extended my own arms and canted forward as if riding an invisible motorcycle. She was right: the sleeves suddenly fit perfectly.

I didn't believe a word of the woman's sales patter – but I thought it was a stroke of genius. Her explanation for the long sleeves seemed to encapsulate all the best techniques for marketing to today's man: the practicality, the attention to detail, the suggestion of a dandyish sense of style combined with a hint of rugged machismo – we were talking *motorbikes*, after all – topped off with an appeal to a faint streak of peacock vanity.

Reader, I bought that shirt. And it began the train of thought that led to the book you've just opened.

THE MANIFOLD MALE

Men are not what they were. Year after year, in article after article, we're told that a new type of man is abroad. His names vary, but certain common characteristics appear each time. He is more sensitive than his predecessors. He is more nurturing, more interested in looking good and – the real point of the message that is being drummed in to us – a lot keener on shopping.

This creature has been with us at least since the 1980s, when glossy magazine journalists dubbed him The New Man. Later he transmogrified into New Lad – who was simply New Man with some of Old Man's nasty habits. And then he evolved into the marketers' ultimate dreamboat: the metrosexual. Here, at last, was the ideal guy. A man who was obsessed with his appearance; who did not hesitate to invest in designer clothes and expensive skincare products; a man who joined designer gyms and lavish spas; a man who was plucked, buffed, toned, tanned and polished to perfection. We didn't hear much about what he read or watched or listened to – we were just told that he consumed.

The term 'metrosexual' was coined – or at least put into print – by the British writer Mark Simpson. His original article appeared in *The Independent* newspaper on 15 November 1994. (The full version can be found on his website, www.marksimpson.com.) The piece refers to an exhibition called 'It's A Man's World', an exhibition of male-oriented brands organized by the British edition of the style magazine *GQ*. Simpson seizes on this as evidence of a new breed of male. 'Traditionally heterosexual men were the world's worst consumers,' he writes. 'All they bought was beer, fags and the occasional Durex, the Wife or Mum bought everything else. In a consumerist world, heterosexual men had no future. So they were replaced by the metrosexual.'

The 1996 shopping list of the metrosexual was as follows: 'Davidoff "Cool Water" aftershave (the one with the naked bodybuilder on the beach), Paul Smith jackets (Ryan Giggs wears them), corduroy shirts (Elvis wore them), chinos (Steve McQueen wore them), motorcycle boots (Marlon Brando wore them), Calvin Klein underwear (Marky Mark wears nothing else). Metrosexual man is a commodity fetishist: a collector of fantasies about the male sold to him by advertising.'

If the metrosexual sounded suspiciously like a homosexual, this was no coincidence. 'Metrosexuality was of course, test-marketed on gay men – with enormous success... It was in the style-obsessed Eighties that the "gay lifestyle" – the single man living in the metropolis and taking himself as his own love-object – became an aspiration for non-homosexuals.'

Duly noted and catalogued, the metrosexual returned for a while to his natural habitat: the pages of men's magazines. But Simpson was surprised in 2003 when he saw 'an American "trendspotter" popping up on telly and in the papers talking excitedly about this exciting new man she'd discovered called a "metrosexual"'. The woman was Marian Salzman, then chief strategy officer at the advertising agency Euro RSCG Worldwide. The agency's report on metrosexuality and marketing to men was making headlines around the world. Salzman – as she fully acknowledged – had updated and commercialized the metrosexual, using him as an avatar for a new, marketing-friendly male. No longer always single, he nonetheless embraced some of the consumption habits that had previously been the preserve of gay men – or of women.

Aided by Salzman's promotional prowess, this far less edgy, infinitely more appealing figure captured the imaginations of journalists, who spilled gallons of ink about him in an outpouring of what Simpson called 'metrosexualmania'. The soccer star David Beckham was inevitably cited as the poster boy for metrosexuality – a married sporting hero who was perfectly at ease with his off-duty role as a fashion icon. Brought forward as further evidence of the metrosexual's existence was the US TV series *Queer Eye for the Straight Guy*, in which straight men gratefully accepted grooming and lifestyle tips from a troupe of gay advisers. Suddenly, the metrosexual had entered popular culture.

I emailed Simpson and asked him how he'd felt about this at the time. He wrote back: 'The marketing fervour around the metrosexual, which began after I introduced him to the US on Salon. com in 2002 [in a piece called "Meet the metrosexual"], appeared to be about selling him to women, not to men. Hence the one doing the selling was a woman herself; hence the way she went on about him "being in touch with his feminine side" and "such a great dad and husband", and that his interest in his appearance was "to please women".'

For Simpson, this interpretation of the metrosexual cast a blind eye over his essential narcissism and turned him into 'New Man' revisited. 'In other words, the marketing version of the metrosexual was too goody-goody to be true. Or be very desirable either. In fact, there is nothing essentially feminine or women-pleasing about metrosexuality at all. Vanity's name is not Woman.'

But the worst part of it, in Simpson's view, was that this distilled version seemed to negate one of the positive achievements of metrosexuality, which was to liberate men from their mothers and wives. 'Metrosexuality actually gives men a certain amount of independence from women: after all, they can actually choose their own clothes, operate a washing machine, and maybe even cook their own food. Whereas the retrosexual depended on women to mother him, the metrosexual mothers himself.'

Both the media and the marketers who had adopted him soon grew tired of the metrosexual. This was in part because he didn't click with consumers. It was a great buzzword, but there were too few metrosexuals in the real world, and even the men who fit into the category didn't like to think of themselves that way. They were just normal guys who used moisturizer and hair gel. In 2006, a study by the advertising agency Leo Burnett Worldwide estimated that only one-fifth of the US population could truly be placed in the 'metrosexual' bracket. And the others didn't aspire to joining them. When male consumers were asked by a Harris poll to name their role models, the top ten responses included Clint Eastwood, Sean Connery and John Wayne ('Metrosexual mortality', *Media Week*, 4 September 2006).

Clearly an alternative had to be found. One option was the 'retro-sexual' – essentially Old Man in all his red-blooded splendour. Watching sport, hanging out with the guys, chucking a steak on the barbecue, chugging beer and letting the stubble sprout at weekends – he was realistic, all right, but not particularly interesting. And certainly not what marketers wanted to hear about.

Fortunately, it looked as though Marian Salzman had come to the rescue again with the übersexual, her latest take on modern masculinity. Now executive vice-president of the advertising agency J. Walter Thompson, she had published a book called *The Future of Men* (2005), along with her colleagues Ira Matathia and Ann O'Reilly. In its pages she suggested that certain men might combine the best of both archetypes – the traditional male values of the retrosexual with the well-groomed stylishness of the metro. 'Compared with the metrosexual, the übersexual is more into relationships than self,' she wrote. 'He dresses for himself more than others (choosing a consistent personal style over fashion fads). Like the metrosexual, the übersexual enjoys shopping, but his approach is more focused; he shops for particular items that enhance his collection rather than shopping as entertainment (he has better things to do than hang out at the mall).'

Once again, we didn't learn a great deal about this latest man's cultural preferences – but at least he still liked shopping. Somehow, though, after an initial flurry of headlines, Herr Über didn't really catch on. Mark Simpson believes this is because he was an adaptation of – rather than a replacement for – the metrosexual. Actually, he was a middle-aged metrosexual. And members of the public, when they referred to a certain type of image-conscious man, still insisted on using the original term.

'That might be because the public is stupid; or it might be because metrosexual actually refers to something observable, it has a sociological or anthropological value – rather than just marketing spin.' Amusingly, Simpson adds a final volley averring that the 'replacement' terms were attempts by marketers to take the gay, narcissistic edge off metrosexuality: 'Ooh! Suits you, sir! So stylish, but not at all vain! No! And really buffed, but not at all gay! Ooh! Heaven forfend, sir!'

MEN WITHOUT WOMEN – AND VICE VERSA

Away from all the semantics, though, what is really going on with men? The truth is that they are different, simply and obviously because society is different. What happened to men, of course, was feminism. A generation of men came home to supper to find that not only was it not on the table, but that the house was empty. Women were still at work, or had decided not to marry after all. Or they had decided to marry much later, leaving men kicking their heels well into their late twenties. Either way, women's assertion of choice had deprived men of their previously clear-cut roles as fathers and breadwinners.

Exploring the vacant rooms of this unfamiliar dwelling, men slowly came to terms with the situation. If women didn't need them as much, maybe that represented a kind of freedom for them, too? Young men who had watched their fathers going through divorces – or collapsing from heart attacks in a welter of overwork and suburban repression – began to wonder if the old archetype was really that attractive in the first place. Others came from single-parent families and had little confidence in the traditional domestic structure. Why not experiment, play the field, take advantage of cheap travel, see if they couldn't get along on their own? 'A gap between the end of adolescence and the onset of adulthood has appeared in a man's early to mid-20s, a period in which no traditional markers of manhood apply and income is almost entirely disposable. These men are left to piece together a male identity armed only with their wallets' ('Man vs. man: did marketing kill the great American Alpha Male?', *Advertising Age*, 13 June 2005). The scene was set, then, for the emergence of the metrosexual.

Soon, though, events took a new turn. Although women had established their right to work, many of them naturally decided that they would also like a supportive partner, and a family. It was time to look for Mr Right. The problem was that, by now, Mr Right was paragliding in the Himalayas, or sitting in his bachelor pad playing video games, or at the gym getting himself toned up for another night on the town. He wasn't ready to lavish all that disposable income on a wife and kids – not just yet. The inability of women in their thirties to find a suitable, responsible man provoked the emergence in popular culture of 'singletons' like Bridget Jones and Carrie from *Sex in the City*.

At the same time, men began wondering whether, having adapted to a gender-neutral society, they hadn't relinquished too much of their masculine heritage – throwing the man, so to speak, out with the bathwater. They weren't at all sure they wanted to emulate the fey, silken-jawed figures they now saw on cinema and television screens – or pouting down at them from advertising billboards. Lacking role models in the real world, they became fascinated by classic celluloid representations of masculinity: the Bogarts and the Waynes, the Eastwoods and the McQueens.

Soon, movies and advertising began to follow their drift. Masculinity re-emerged with a touch of 21st century irony and a dash of metro-inspired sensitivity. The new James Bond – as portrayed by Daniel Craig – was an altogether craggier and more brutal incarnation than his predecessor, but he allowed himself to fall in love with his female companion. Bond's rival for action movie supremacy was Jason Bourne (Matt Damon) – the amnesiac assassin from *The Bourne Identity* (2002) and its sequels. With his sharp crew-cut, laconic dialogue and impressive martial arts skills, Bourne is not remotely feminized; yet he is also vulnerable and conflicted. Bruce Willis returned in 2007 for another of the *Die Hard* films, in which he a plays no-nonsense cop. In *Live Free or Die Hard*, he spends most of the film trying to save his daughter. The rugged features of British actor Clive Owen appeared on print ads for Lancôme skincare products. And it seems unfair not to mention George Clooney, who with his silvery hair and elegant suits is a polished version of the iconic male – a throwback to matinee idols of the past.

These figures reflected the self-exploration that was going on in the real world. In fact, it often resembled a backlash. Examining the destiny of men in his 2006 book, *Manliness*, Harvard professor of government Harvey C. Mansfield put his cards firmly on the table. 'Manliness is still around, and we still find it attractive,' he asserted. '[C]onsider the evidence for manliness in social psychology and evolutionary biology, which show as best they can that the stereotypes of men and women are basically correct... Manliness favours war, likes risk, and admires heroes... Manliness is sometimes vulnerable and fragile but doesn't care to admit human weaknesses.' His book was emphatically black-and-white, right down to the cover. Women, he argued, still wanted manly men. Men may not have been perfect, but they endured. Then one imagines him sitting back and waiting for the indignant emails to fly.

And yet, responses from both men and women tended toward the dismissive. Mansfield was a 'conservative' – what could you expect? 'Mansfield seems stuck in a semantic time warp,' commented *The New York Times* ('Who's the man?', 19 March 2006). But Mansfield's book was relevant precisely *because* it was old-fashioned. The disinterring of old-school masculinity was well underway. Lori Borgman, who wrote a syndicated column for Knight Ridder newspapers, had reacted savagely to a 2005 book by Maureen Dowd, called *Are Men Necessary?*. 'There are a lot of things I sometimes think I'd like to be, but a man is never one of them. Talk about a group maligned, vilified and marginalized. For the most part...men are stand-up guys. They work hard. They create, tinker, build, engineer and achieve. They take carping, criticizing and complaining on the chin, and rarely get the thanks they deserve. Last year in our nation, 1.5 million babies were born out of wedlock. These children have no "man of the house", no dad who wants to marry mom…Are men necessary? Very much so. It is a tragedy we have spent so long telling them they weren't.' ('Yes…men are necessary', 2 December 2005.)

Other articles appeared suggesting that women did not, after all, desire men who looked prettier than they did. Many men were undoubtedly cheered by this news – particularly those who'd thought of themselves as 'old-school' all along. When I mentioned the subject of this book to a fifty-something acquaintance, he said, 'Just tell advertising agencies to stop portraying us as Photoshopped buffoons.' Always happy to pick up on a trend, the media began talking of a 'menaissance'. Perhaps there was a place for old-fashioned masculinity in a gender-neutral society. Maybe we could have our moisturizer and our power drills too.

WHAT LIES AHEAD

As I walked out of the store with the bag containing my new shirt, I began to turn this state of affairs over in my mind. Was the metrosexual really a myth, or had men become rampant consumers? Should advertisers try to appeal to traditional masculinity, or some new, evolved form of manliness? Weren't, in fact, all men different – depending on their age, their status, and even the hour of the day? What attitudes, if any, did they all have in common? What were the triggers that motivated men to buy?

Coincidentally, my interest was further piqued by a telephone call from Margaret Jobling, who had just taken charge of men's grooming brands at Unilever. She, too, was interested in finding out what made men tick as consumers. I felt the most sensible way of doing that would be to take several male-oriented brands and look at their marketing strategies, in the hope of spotting similarities among those that worked best. I was also keen to find out how brands had adapted to men's transformed lifestyles and attitudes.

As I didn't want to concentrate purely on fashion and skincare – the two areas, arguably, in which men's consumption patterns have changed the most – I decided to take a day in the life of a man and find out how he engaged with brands at different stages of his journey. To entertain myself (and hopefully you, too) I decided to open each chapter with a snapshot of a fictional 'branded male'. He is a caricature – but not entirely. Some of his habits are my own, some have been stolen from friends, and others still were gleaned from the marketers I interviewed for the main text.

While recounting his adventures, though, I was well aware that my branded male hailed from a very narrow segment of society. Many men, I am sure, are immune to constant exhortations to consume. Before I'd even begun the first chapter, I received the following email from my father. In it he described himself as 'one of the oldest branded males on the planet'. He continued, 'The fragrance I'm wearing is a heady blend of liniment, Old Spice and Savlon, mixed with the aroma of garden compost and car polish. My clothes closely resemble the ones I wore in 1978, 1988 and 1998: surely Fair Isle cardigans and flannel slacks will come back into fashion soon?'

He was only partly joking. This, dear readers, is what you are up against. But don't despair – on the next page you'll meet a considerably more willing male consumer.

1

Skin

Scene One: The Bathroom

The shelf below his bathroom mirror is a battlefield. Occasionally he tries to blame his girlfriend, but the truth is that half the items fighting for territory on the strip of zinc are his. The ranks of grey, white and black vessels resemble advancing chess pieces. Their provenance is mysterious: he wouldn't be able to tell you exactly when Kiehl's Blue Herbal Astringent Lotion and Clarins Active Face Wash insinuated themselves into his morning routine. Not to mention Clinique M Lotion and American Crew Classic Wax. He certainly didn't rush out and buy them all at once. It was a slow accretion; a steady assault on his subconscious until each of these products seemed essential. It hardly seems possible that there was a time when a razor, foam, water and soap would have sufficed, followed by a quick blast of deodorant.

He hits the shower, sloughing off the dead skin cells – invisible to the eye, but the magazines assure him that they exist – with an exfoliating scrub from Kiehl's. Then he washes with Anthony Logistics Shower Gel. After that, his hair gets the treatment with Kérastase Frequent Use Shampoo, 'to help reduce the risk of hair loss', because he's 35 and you can't be too careful. When he's rinsed out the shampoo, he applies a sneaky lick of his girlfriend's Garnier Fructis Fortifying Conditioner. The French on the packaging nudges him into thinking about his business trip to Paris later that day.

The conditioner follows the shampoo down the drain and he cuts the water, stepping onto the bathmat.

He's not out of the bathroom yet, though. Turning to the over-crowded shelf once again, he selects Biotherm Homme Sensitive Skin Shaving Foam. And then he reaches for his razor. This is a thing of beauty: an old-fashioned 'safety' razor of the type his grandfather once used. It was a gift from his girlfriend, and after a few nasty incidents early on – beads of blood appearing at his Adam's apple – he's learned to handle it with aplomb.

Like many men of his generation, he started out using an electric razor in imitation of his father. But he never really liked its hot buzzing against his skin, and so he switched to a blade. Until recently, he used the Gillette Sensor Excel with two blades. He was about to upgrade to the triple-bladed Gillette Mach3 Turbo when his birthday came along, and with it a step back into shaving history. The supposedly primitive – yet undeniably masculine – safety razor has a snobbish appeal. Indeed, he scoffed at the recent news that Gillette was launching a razor with no less than *five* blades. He remains on the Gillette marketing radar, however, as the rectangular blades he buys for the safety razor are still made by the company.

After he's finished shaving, he applies the Kiehl's astringent to the couple of nicks he's picked up. Then he moisturises with the Clinique lotion – which beneath its urbane silver-grey livery is little different to the brand's moisturizer for women. The final touch is a dab of Hugo Boss Baldessarini aftershave, once again chosen by his girlfriend. He fixes his hair with the American Crew Classic Wax, aiming for a carefully dishevelled look.

He peers critically at himself in the mirror. There are dark, faintly puffy rings under his eyes, the result of long hours at a computer screen and one pint too many in the pub last night. Frowning, he selects a tube of Nickel Eye Contour Lift from the shelf and gingerly applies it.

His conditioning is almost total.

THE GROOMING CONUNDRUM

Although our hero is not unique, male personal care is a far smaller sector than the beauty industry would like it to be. In 2005, market analyst Datamonitor predicted that sales of grooming products for men in Europe and the United States would grow from US$31.6 billion in 2003 to nearly US$40 billion in 2010. The women's beauty industry is already estimated to be worth around US$100 billion worldwide (Future Body Visions Summit, 20–21 September 2006). If men are beginning to rival women in the vanity stakes, it seems they're still nervous about putting their wallets where their wrinkles are.

Another research group, Mintel, said starkly in a 2006 report: 'Men's toiletries have failed to achieve the explosive growth anticipated since the late 1980s, when… manufacturer Shulton launched its Insignia men's range, the first integrated line offering men top-to-toe grooming options. This was supposed to herald the emergence of the New Man, but the reality was that most men were not ready to embrace the concept of a multi-product grooming regime. Instead, it has been a much longer and slower process, highlighting the reality that men will never adopt the levels of interest and investment in the toiletries industry that is fuelling the women's beauty industry.' (Men's Toiletries UK, March 2006.) Nonetheless, the market is growing. Yet another researcher, Euromonitor, claims that the total UK market for men's grooming products – including fragrances and basics like soap and shampoo – rose by 33.2 per cent between 2001 and 2006.

The world's best-selling male grooming product is Unilever's Axe (known in the United Kingdom as Lynx), which started life as a deodorant before successfully expanding into other personal care niches. But Axe is aimed at younger men – adolescents, primarily – and Unilever admits that it is a long way off cracking the broader men's market.

'Male grooming is a manufacturer's term that means little to the average man on the street,' says Margaret Jobling, male grooming global brand director at Unilever. 'At best it's shorthand for preening – and at worst it's seen as effeminate. Product development is not the problem. Today there are products designed to tackle almost every male concern, from anti-ageing moisturizer to abdomen-firming cream. The problem lies in engaging with men using the appropriate language and persuading them to try new things.'

Yet there is little disagreement that men are changing. We may dismiss the metrosexual and his successors – the retrosexual, the übersexual and so on – as media phenomena fabricated by the advertising industry; but there is plenty of evidence that men in the real world are becoming more concerned with their appearance. 'Today's men are far more likely to adopt a regular grooming routine consisting of shave, shower, deodorise, hair styling and fragrance than ever before,' confirms Mintel, almost grudgingly.

Simply because men perspire more than women, selling them deodorant has never been much of a problem. Marketing fragrance has proved marginally more challenging, although most men now have a favourite aftershave or cologne. Research in the UK, carried out by TNS for *The Grocer* magazine, suggests that fragrance sales are driving 'the lion's share' of the male cosmetics market, taking a 37.4 per cent share of the sector – with sales up by 19 per cent to £208 million in 2006. This is impressive given that men are notoriously averse to testing new brands. It's also tough persuading them to try anything beyond the conventional masculine odours of lime, leather or musk: particularly the former, as 21st century men like to smell tangy and well-scrubbed.

At its most obvious, marketing fragrance to men is based around the power of attraction. It's a furrow that Lynx/Axe has ploughed with irony and innovation. Not all brands have such highly developed wit. When a fragrance called Addiction was re-launched in the UK in the autumn of 2006, its marketing targeted 17 to 27-year-old males out 'on the pull'. The slogan was 'Can't get enough', and there were nationwide sampling activities at nightclubs and student unions ('Addiction relaunched with "masstige" focus', *The Grocer*, 26 August 2006).

But signs of increasing sophistication have emerged. *The New York Times* recently suggested that gender distinctions in the fragrance sector were breaking down, resulting in a new array of 'gender-free' scents. But it also admitted that buyers of these, though influential, were 'a small (and sometimes persnickety) clan'. 'I don't want to show up at the party in Drakkar or Obsession, something that I wore in puberty,' one customer was quoted as saying ('Scent of a person', 23 March 2006).

Gender-free fragrances have something in common with Calvin Klein's CK One, launched in 1994 as a 'unisex' scent. It proved highly successful with younger consumers, and in 2007 the company launched a sequel called CKin2u. Like its predecessor, it was aimed at vaguely trendy kids in their late teens or early twenties, who are less concerned by gender distinctions and think more in terms of the social group. Creed's Original Santal, on the other hand, was launched as a gender-free fragrance for discerning adults. Its advertising showed a ring of bottles and the line 'For men and women'.

Traditional fragrance advertising, as we all know, features a handsome, obviously successful male. His duty is to appeal not to men, but to women – who buy fragrances for their partners and urge them to experiment. But soccer star David Beckham – the celebrity most closely linked to the 'metrosexuality' phenomenon – clearly felt that men were ready to take matters into their own hands when he launched a branded scent called David Beckham's

Instinct in 2005. Although the response was mixed, the strategy was clear: a strong role model might encourage a man to adopt a new brand.

Jobling accepts that the plethora of men's style magazines, along with the influence of the gay market and straight male icons like Beckham, have encouraged men to linger in front of their mirrors. But she doubts that they will ever be as keen on beauty products as women. 'The simple fact is that men are wired differently,' she says. 'A lot of beauty marketing is about the power of attraction. But what do women look for in men? They look for financial stability, emotional strength, loyalty, security and, yes, a good sense of humour. Shiny hair and soft skin are a long way down the list. And what are men looking for? They're looking for fecundity: a sexual partner. Women are obsessed with looking good because that's how men see them.'

Related to this is the challenge of encouraging men to open up about their looks. Women have never been afraid to comment on the beauty of others: 'I love that actress – she's gorgeous.' But few straight men would feel comfortable acknowledging the handsomeness of a fellow male. And so the advertising of beauty products aimed at men must promise to keep them looking 'toned' and 'fit' and smelling 'fresh'.

Enter Genevieve Flaven, of the French trend-tracking organization Style-Vision, who has another outlook. 'Men have entered a great period of exploration,' she believes. 'They want to remain loyal to certain male values, but they are playing with new interpretations of masculinity. And brands have seen a way of tapping in to the multiple facets of this new man.'

French giant L'Oréal is one of a growing number of beauty companies convinced by the potential of the male sector. It markets a range of skincare products under the L'Oréal Paris Men Expert label. At the time of writing, this embraced everything from 'skin renovating' washes to 'hydro energetic' bronzer (we'll return to the arcane language of men's grooming products later). Clarins also has a range for men, featuring the now familiar moisturizing lotions along with fake tan and 'the first hand care treatment specifically for men'. Lancôme has a similar line – and signed up rugged British actor Clive Owen to promote it in January 2007. This was the first time a male Hollywood star had become the face of a skincare range. Lancôme said its 'clinical research' among males aged from 19 to 70 proved that men were concerned about dehydrated skin due to shaving, as well as loss of skin firmness as they grew older. Men also worried about bags under their eyes, pores and age spots, the company insisted.

Estée Lauder was a pioneer in the sector, creating the Clinique Skin Supplies for Men range in 1976, and the Aramis LabSeries line ten years later. One of Clinique's more forward-thinking products was 'M Cover' – a 'natural-look cover for dark circles and blemishes'. Note the delicate tiptoeing around the word 'concealer', which has feminine associations. Usually, when it comes to selling skincare to men, marketers don't stray too far from the blade.

THE RAZOR'S EDGE

'Everything begins with shaving,' confirms Genevieve Flaven of Style-Vision. 'It's the ultimate male ritual – the big "man moment" of the day. And this ritual can be used as a fulcrum for selling men a host of other products, from moisturizers and anti-ageing creams to fragrances and bronzing lotions. If a subtle link with the shaving ritual can be established, the products take on a masculine image and the consumer doesn't feel feminized.'

The ultimate shaving brand, of course, is Gillette. It dominates the shaving and razor business, with a 70 per cent slice of the market. Although it came under attack from aspiring rivals in the 1990s, its position was strengthened when it was purchased in 2005 – for US$54 billion – by Procter & Gamble. It is now part of a distinctly masculine division within P&G, which embraces everything from Braun electric razors to Duracell alkaline batteries. P&G sees plenty of synergies in the Gillette acquisition: 'We have the best-selling male fragrance in Hugo Boss,' a P&G senior executive told *Time* magazine, shortly after the merger: 'How about a Hugo Boss designer razor?' ('Land of the Giants', 31 January 2005.)

Gillette's famous advertising slogan is, of course, 'The best a man can get'. Amusingly, though, the company was started by a man whose middle name was 'Camp'.

King Camp Gillette was born in Fond du Lac, Wisconsin, in 1855. His entry in the MIT archive suggests that he had invention in his genes: his father was a 'some-time patent agent and inveterate tinkerer', while his mother's experiments in the kitchen eventually yielded a cookbook (MIT Inventor Archive: http://web.mit.edu/invent).

Gillette became a travelling salesman at the age of 17, and by the 1890s he was working for a razor company. At that time, men were still using cut-throat razors, which had to be sharpened on a leather strop. As he was constantly on the road, Gillette knew how impractical and dangerous these devices could be. He hit upon the idea of a 'safety' razor that used disposable blades, which could be thrown away when they became dull. While the razor itself would be priced lower than its competitors, the manufacturer would make a profit out of the disposable blades, which would be stamped with his brand. The problem was convincing anybody that there was enough of a market to support the research and development costs of conjuring fingernail-thin blades out of sheet steel. Metallurgists at MIT assured him that this was technically impossible.

Gillette's own personality can't have helped his quest, as he must have come across as a rather eccentric sort of dreamer. A utopian socialist, in 1894 he'd written a book called *The Human Drift*, decrying society's obsession with money. He proposed that the 'monstrous, sprawling' cities created by the industrial revolution be replaced by hive-like communities protected by glass domes. Although these views seem to have been provoked by his own feeling of under-achievement as his career stalled, he clung to them even when his invention made him a millionaire.

After several false starts, Gillette recruited engineer William Emery Nickerson, and together they refined the production process. In 1901 they founded The American Safety Razor Company, which changed its name to The Gillette Safety Razor Company a year later (World Advertising Research Centre company profile in association with Adbrands, February 2007). By now, Gillette was in his late forties.

In 1903, Gillette sold only 51 razors and 168 blades. To give the razors a push, Gillette began offering them free of charge for a short period, figuring that he could sell plenty of blades once he got consumers hooked. At the same time, he launched a major advertising drive. By the end of the following year, sales had rocketed to nearly 100,000 razors and more than 120,000 blades. Gillette became a marketing phenomenon. Over the next five years, sales quadrupled and the company expanded into Canada, France, Germany and the United Kingdom. Although Gillette's invention had been patented in 1904, competitors inevitably emerged. The company's standard response was to gobble them up. The final nail in the coffin for the barbershop shave came with the First World War, when the US government issued 3.5 million Gillette razors and 36 million blades to the military. As a way of developing brand loyalty, this was hard to beat.

Not that Gillette could have been accused of laxity when it came to marketing matters. From the very start, his own face and signature were printed onto the wrappers containing his blades, transforming him into a sort of celebrity: one of the original brand icons. In the 1920s the company ran a joint promotion with banks, deploying the slogan 'Save and Shave!' Ironically, in 1929 King C. Gillette became a victim of the Wall Street Crash, which wiped out almost the entirety of his fortune. At the same time, boardroom machinations had slowly forced him out of the business, until he found himself ousted by the company he had created. He died bitter and almost penniless at the age of 77, in 1934, after an unsuccessful last-ditch bid to extract oil from shale.

But the company survived and prospered. After the Second World War it began to diversify, launching its Foamy shaving cream in 1953. It also embarked on the first of a series of acquisitions. Fearing for the future of the disposable blade in the face of the new electric razor, Gillette cannily bought Braun in 1967 for US$68 million. Later acquisitions included toothbrush maker Oral-B (1984), luxury pen maker Waterman (1987), Parker Pens (1993) and Duracell (1996). With Braun, Duracell today sits in a 'blades and razors and powered products' business division within P&G.

Rather like Nike, which seems determined to endow joggers with superhuman powers, Gillette underpins its marketing with constant technological advancements. The current cycle began as early as 1967, when Gillette invented a razor called the Techmatic, whose 'system' meant that users no longer had to handle naked blades. In 1971, Gillette launched the first twin-bladed razor, the GII. This was followed by the swivel-headed Contour in 1984 and the Sensor in 1991 – the first razor to feature spring-mounted blades. The problem for Gillette is that each technical leap costs more money than the last. For example, according to the World Advertising Research Centre (WARC), Gillette spent ten years and more than US$150 million on research before launching the Sensor. The Mach3, launched in 2000, soaked up US$750 million, plus advertising spend of US$250 million. It's not surprising that the company felt compelled to dive into the protective arms of P&G.

Despite the expense involved, Gillette may feel obliged to continue its marketing-by-technology strategy, because 'functionality' and 'performance' are among the strongest buying motors among male consumers. But the company flirted with ridiculousness in

2006 with the launch of the Gillette F... no less than six blades – if you count... Even the most marketing-sensitive consu... whether six blades were really necessa... had been doing the job for years, weren't... to encourage the others?

In fact, there are signs that the brand m... ...away from technology and towards sponsorship. In 2003 it signed a US$20 million marketing deal with NASCAR (The National Association for Stock Car Auto Racing), which has an almost religious following in the United States (see Chapter 10). A year later, it signed up soccer star David Beckham for a three-year endorsement deal. Beckham chose not to renew the contract when it ran out, having apparently been advised to push for a profit share in his endorsement arrangements, rather than accepting a flat fee ('Beckham and Gillette part company after talks fail', Brandrepublic.com, 5 July 2007). In the meantime, Gillette had pushed ahead and signed up Tiger Woods, Thierry Henry and Roger Federer for a global campaign entitled 'Champions'. The company's press release, issued from its Boston headquarters on 4 February 2007, said it all: 'The three ambassadors will be fully integrated into Gillette brand programs and will be leveraged through multifaceted marketing initiatives, including global print and broadcast advertising, consumer promotions, point-of-sale materials, online and public relations in support of Gillette premium shaving products.'

The access to big bucks and star firepower is crucial, because Gillette is under constant attack from its competitors. Schick – which owns Wilkinson Sword in Europe – has been at its throat for years. Schick has taken Gillette to court in both Europe and the United States arguing that the 'best a man can get' claim is no longer true, and that the company's advertising is therefore misleading. The accusations have never gone the distance, but they sting.

time being, though, Gillette can feel confident of its
on as one of the few genuinely global male-oriented brands.
its first year as a division of P&G, it sold US$3.5 billion worth
of blades and razors, with net earnings of US$781 million. It has
also proved adept at marketing male skincare products around
the shaving ritual, launching 'pre- and post-shave' gels and balms
to accompany each of its razors. Both the Mach3 and the Fusion
models came with a 'family' of tie-in potions to help consumers
achieve the perfect shave. They were also supported by websites
offering shaving tips, just in case men hadn't got the hang of the
task.

SHOP OPTIONS

Along with functionality, familiarity is another important driver
when it comes to male personal care shopping. That's where
Gillette wins. Few men are as experimental as our hero, who
enjoys trying out different brands until he finds the product that
is perfectly suited to the task. Older male consumers – in their
thirties and upwards – are generally more stuck in their ways.
They dislike browsing in the skincare section, so they just buy
whatever they bought before – or a declination of the same. Men
take a SWAT approach to shopping: get in, do the job, and get the
hell out.

Retailers are keen to change this behaviour. A typical initiative is
that of the Bijenkorf department store in Amsterdam. Its research
revealed that two-thirds of its customers were female, and that
the men who entered the store were mainly along for the ride with
their wives and girlfriends, rather than out to shop for themselves.
In a bid to attract them, the store created a stand-alone men's
section combining clothes, accessories, skincare and gadgets ('It's
different for guys', *Financial Times*, 28 April 2007). It realized
that men, with their search-and-destroy shopping methods, would
prefer to find all their stuff in one place rather than being forced
to hike from one aisle to another.

2006 with the launch of the Gillette Fusion, which incorporated no less than six blades – if you counted the sideburn trimmer. Even the most marketing-sensitive consumer must have wondered whether six blades were really necessary. If three cutting edges had been doing the job for years, weren't the extra three just there to encourage the others?

In fact, there are signs that the brand may shift its focus away from technology and towards sponsorship. In 2003 it signed a US$20 million marketing deal with NASCAR (The National Association for Stock Car Auto Racing), which has an almost religious following in the United States (see Chapter 10). A year later, it signed up soccer star David Beckham for a three-year endorsement deal. Beckham chose not to renew the contract when it ran out, having apparently been advised to push for a profit share in his endorsement arrangements, rather than accepting a flat fee ('Beckham and Gillette part company after talks fail', Brandrepublic.com, 5 July 2007). In the meantime, Gillette had pushed ahead and signed up Tiger Woods, Thierry Henry and Roger Federer for a global campaign entitled 'Champions'. The company's press release, issued from its Boston headquarters on 4 February 2007, said it all: 'The three ambassadors will be fully integrated into Gillette brand programs and will be leveraged through multifaceted marketing initiatives, including global print and broadcast advertising, consumer promotions, point-of-sale materials, online and public relations in support of Gillette premium shaving products.'

The access to big bucks and star firepower is crucial, because Gillette is under constant attack from its competitors. Schick – which owns Wilkinson Sword in Europe – has been at its throat for years. Schick has taken Gillette to court in both Europe and the United States arguing that the 'best a man can get' claim is no longer true, and that the company's advertising is therefore misleading. The accusations have never gone the distance, but they sting.

For the time being, though, Gillette can feel confident of its position as one of the few genuinely global male-oriented brands. In its first year as a division of P&G, it sold US$3.5 billion worth of blades and razors, with net earnings of US$781 million. It has also proved adept at marketing male skincare products around the shaving ritual, launching 'pre- and post-shave' gels and balms to accompany each of its razors. Both the Mach3 and the Fusion models came with a 'family' of tie-in potions to help consumers achieve the perfect shave. They were also supported by websites offering shaving tips, just in case men hadn't got the hang of the task.

SHOP OPTIONS

Along with functionality, familiarity is another important driver when it comes to male personal care shopping. That's where Gillette wins. Few men are as experimental as our hero, who enjoys trying out different brands until he finds the product that is perfectly suited to the task. Older male consumers – in their thirties and upwards – are generally more stuck in their ways. They dislike browsing in the skincare section, so they just buy whatever they bought before – or a declination of the same. Men take a SWAT approach to shopping: get in, do the job, and get the hell out.

Retailers are keen to change this behaviour. A typical initiative is that of the Bijenkorf department store in Amsterdam. Its research revealed that two-thirds of its customers were female, and that the men who entered the store were mainly along for the ride with their wives and girlfriends, rather than out to shop for themselves. In a bid to attract them, the store created a stand-alone men's section combining clothes, accessories, skincare and gadgets ('It's different for guys', *Financial Times*, 28 April 2007). It realized that men, with their search-and-destroy shopping methods, would prefer to find all their stuff in one place rather than being forced to hike from one aisle to another.

Research from the United States supports the theory that men hate asking for directions. In a report called *The Lost Male Shoppers*, America's Research Group revealed that men were deserting department stores in their droves, particularly during the key Christmas period. It conducted 72,000 shopper interviews over 12 consecutive Christmas seasons. 'In the past decade, the number of men shopping at major department stores dropped gradually, but consistently, from 23 per cent to the current level of 7 per cent' (*Research Review*, Vol. 13, No. 1, 2006). One of the reasons given for this was the shrinking of the stores' electronics departments, which drove men to seek specialist technology stores. But 23 per cent of men also reported that they found department stores 'confusing and difficult to shop'. Contradictorily, although they are shy about asking the way, men demand good service when they get there. No less than 45 per cent of the men surveyed said that they'd abandoned department stores because 'no-one was available to assist them with their purchases'. When they finally needed advice, the only visible employee was operating the cash register.

Usefully, ARG suggests luring men back to department stores with 'men's shopping evenings' or other male-oriented events tailored 'to the male segment of the credit-card base'.

When the Miami branch of Macy's department store opened a 'treatment world' for men at the end of 2004, *The Miami Herald* provided an enlightened commentary on the trends behind the decision. 'Cosmetics have always been big business for department stores,' it observed. 'Cosmetics and toiletry companies rang up US\$31.1 billion in US sales last year... Growth in the sector, however, has been slowing. The 2003 sales figure represents a paltry 1.7 percent gain over the prior year. Sales of men's cosmetics and anti-aging skin care products, in contrast, are sporting double-digit gains.' Tucked away in the newsprint, we also find the reason that brands and retailers would like us to become paranoid about ageing. 'Cosmetics are good business for department stores because high-end anti-aging products can yield large profit margins.' ('Cosmetics firms eye male market', 23 October 2004.)

Tempting men to hang around rather than taking their usual hit-and-run approach is becoming a popular strategy. In New York, Bloomingdale's has added 'seating, sports magazines and televisions to the men's areas to help stressed-out shoppers to relax'. Harrods in London has had a barber for years. In Paris, the owners of one department store have cunningly established a link between home improvements and fashion. For years, Parisian men have enjoyed hanging out in the basement of the BHV store (it stands for *Bazaar de l'Hôtel de Ville* – the store by the town hall). The vast space is famously devoted to DIY equipment of all kinds, and men spend happy hours down there fingering drill bits and comparing grades of sandpaper. In a stroke of genius, the store's owners turned an empty warehouse nearby into a male fashion and grooming emporium called BHV Homme. The pared-down, loft-style space includes four floors of clothing and accessories, a traditional barber, a personal care department and a small spa where customers can get a manicure, a massage or a facial. There's also a café with an agreeable terrace. At a stroke, BHV obtained a monopoly on 'manly' activities in that part of town.

Stand-alone men's concept stores continue to emerge. In November 2006 a store called Wholeman, entirely devoted to male personal care – or as it says, 'body maintenance for men' – opened at 67 New Bond Street in London. Its chairman is Bob Ager, who has previously worked in a marketing capacity for the department stores Selfridges in London and Lane Crawford in Hong Kong. Ager explains that considerable qualitative research was done to refine the concept. 'I've rarely seen a concept so endorsed by respondents,' he says. 'At the outset we felt that it was mostly likely to appeal to younger guys who loosely fit into the group referred to as "metrosexuals", but what came out of the research and what experience has shown us is that interest in the category is far broader than you might imagine.'

Like BHV Homme in Paris, Wholeman also offers spa treatments alongside its range of products. 'Most retailers haven't really grasped how to sell to men,' he says. 'In department stores, cosmetics and skincare are organised by brand, and all the brands want separate stands, so the men's products end up alongside the women's. But a women's perfume department is an alien environment to men. They just don't want to be there.'

Initially, Ager and Wholeman's backers toyed with the idea of an all-embracing men's store, with gadgets and 'boys' toys' alongside the grooming products. But the research showed that men preferred a more targeted offer. 'They liked the idea of a grooming one-stop-shop, where they could buy products but also get a facial.'

Wholeman will expand into other cities, although Ager emphasizes that he does not see it as a high street brand. 'We'll be aiming for sophisticated urban environments. Men are coming round to grooming – and the media has been very supportive – but probably only about 20 per cent of guys are seriously into it at the moment. That leaves a big market to win over.'

NATIONAL CHARACTERISTICS

British men are more experimental than other Europeans – and approaches to grooming definitely vary by country. In Germany, for example, local giant Beiersdorf dominates the market with its Nivea for Men range. This was officially launched in 1986, although Nivea had been making male-oriented products since 1922, when it launched a shaving soap. A national interest in health and wellness and the equation of smooth looks with success mean that German men are naturally disposed to grooming regimes, shying away from the stubbly, nonchalant look that lurks in the corridors of many French companies. Beiersdorf has successfully taken the brand around the world – recently launching a 'whitening cream' for men in India, where it believes the male grooming market is about to explode. (Indian women have long yearned for fairer skin for complex reasons that relate to both the caste system and, perhaps, the vestiges of colonial rule.)

In the United States, the internet is a popular method of targeting men, many of whom still feel uncomfortable shopping for skin-care products. Male interest websites like Askmen.com are flourishing, and brands regularly run print ads and e-mail campaigns directing men to online shopping sites. In early 2007, Nivea for Men promoted its Energizing Hydro Gel moisturizer via a campaign called 'Up 4 anything'. Sponsored by the men's magazine *Maxim*, as well as rock music bible *Rolling Stone* and sports channel ESPN, it encouraged men to log on to a website and post videos of themselves explaining why they should win a trip to Las Vegas.

Around the same time, Philips Norelco launched a US campaign for its body hair razor for men, the Bodygroom, via a website. It was a sensitive issue, as men were reluctant to talk about their desire to trim their underarm hair, tidy up their chest hair, remove back hair, and perhaps prune other, more delicate regions. The online ad was simple – a cool, funny guy in a bathrobe explained why you should shave your body hair (the 'adds an optical inch' argument was particularly compelling), supported by amusing visual innuendoes involving vegetables. The razors whizzed out of stores, the campaign created a new category, and after research the company found that 60 per cent of purchasers did so because of the site (www.shaveeverywhere.com).

As we've seen, the growth of the male grooming sector is by no means a purely Western phenomenon. Lancôme, for one, is convinced that it is an international trend. It claims that a survey of 20,000 men around the world showed that European men use skincare to 'be at their best – dynamic,' while US consumers want to be at 'a business and social advantage'. Japanese men want to 'feel confident and look younger'.

Men in many Asian cultures have long been comfortable with grooming rituals, so the adoption of more recent skincare aids should not be a great leap. An article in *The Wall Street Journal* noted: 'Cosmetics marketers are tapping into a powerful shift in gender images taking place in many developed East Asian countries; the conservative, macho male stereotypes that have long dominated society in Japan and South Korea are giving way to a softer, more gender-neutral look.' It observed that 'as women gain power and influence, they are expressing a preference for different kinds of men'. For example, South Korean women are apparently attracted to men with 'a pretty face, big eyes and fair skin', which is encouraging men to turn to cosmetics to help them fulfil the ideal ('Asia's lipstick lads', *Wall Street Journal*, 27 May 2005).

A year earlier, the Manila arm of research company Synovate had published the results of a 'male vanity' study conducted among 3,000 men across the Philippines, China, Hong Kong, Korea, Singapore and Taiwan. Among other findings, it suggested that 67 per cent of Filipino men used fragrances – by far the highest in the region – followed by Koreans at 28 per cent. Koreans were more concerned about their hair, with 53 per cent saying they used some kind of styling product. The popularity of skin cleansers was low, but 67 per cent of Korean men admitted to using a moisturizer 'perhaps... because of their chilly winter weather', the article ventured. ('Vanity, thy name is man', *BusinessWorld*, 27 December 2004.)

A few months later, a piece in *Time Asia* confirmed that the metro-sexual had definitely arrived in the region. 'Narcissism is in, thanks to economic growth, higher disposable incomes, shifting gender roles, and fashion and cosmetics industries eager to expand their customer bases,' it declared ('Mirror, mirror... ', October 2005). The piece suggested that the image-obsessed male had become a 'recognizable sub-species' in many Asian markets. 'In China, they are called the *aimei nanren* (love beauty men), fastidious fellows who are unafraid to spend a few hours in a beauty salon getting pedicures, pore packs and back waxes. Their counterparts in Korea are the *kkotminam* (flower men), club-hopping packs of primping fops who accessorize with designer bling and faux fur.' The article pointed out that the Isetan department store in Tokyo had installed a whole floor devoted to men's cosmetics. 'Dandy House, Japan's leading chain of men's beauty salons (with 59 outlets), got its start in the 1980s because its founders noticed how women were pressuring men to adopt better grooming habits.'

Once again, women were portrayed as the puppet-mistresses behind the feminized man. Others have ascribed the new interest in grooming to a collective admiration for former Prime Minister Junichiro Koizumi, who stepped down from office in September 2006. 'With his Beethoven locks, thin build, and dapper choice of suits, Koizumi was something of a heartthrob with women voters... ' ('Japan raises the male beauty bar', *BusinessWeek*, 11 December 2006). As in Germany, looking presentable has become linked with power and success. By 2006 the men's beauty care market in Japan had doubled since the turn of the millennium, raking in US$248 million a year, according to Yano Research Institute in Tokyo. That same year the Japanese cosmetics giant Shiseido released a survey claiming that more than 70 per cent of male respondents thought it was important to take care of their appearance.

TOOLED UP

With most men still wary of marketing that contains any hint of narcissism, skincare brands are playing it safe. The harnessing of male icons, as discussed above, is an increasingly sure route. The promise of practical results is another.

While Axe had successfully played since its 1983 launch on the idea of 'The Axe Effect' – a scent that makes its wearer irresistible to women – it had problems expanding into the shower gel market, because users felt that any potential effect was literally washed down the drain. Brand owner Unilever and its advertising agency Bartle Bogle Hegarty tackled this challenge by re-booting the functionality factor. Its marketing strategy suggested that seduction was not just about dousing one's body in scent, but required an entire preparatory process – similar to the way that athletes get in shape for major events. Thus it introduced four products: Groove, which charges your body and puts you in the mood for 'a legendary night'; Reload, which re-energises, so you're ready to go out; Sunrise, which stimulates the senses; and Contact, which moisturises the skin so 'you are ready for close contact'. Later products moved the story on to the following morning, with an invigorating anti-hangover gel and a scrub that 'removed traces of a filthy night'. ('Axe – Getting Dirty Boys Clean', IPA Effectiveness Awards, 2006.)

Positioning grooming products as tools – or even medicines – is the most common method of promoting personal care to men. For confirmation, one only needs to look at the language on the packaging. The Swiss brand Task Essential – which already has a solid masculine ring about it – includes in its range products such as Oxywater O² Oxygen Spray and Stop Burning aftershave. LabSeries Skincare for Men is another example. 'High tech, high performance, high results,' says its website, which assures us that, 'since 1987, the elite team of doctors, scientists and skin care specialists of the LabSeries Research Center' has been striving away to develop innovative products that will enable us to look our best. Its products include 'Mega Foam Shave', 'Skin Refinisher' and 'Root Power Hair Tonic'. You can practically hear the products growling. In all these cases, colours are either primary and assertive, like an emergency vehicle, or soothing and neutral, like a laboratory or a gymnasium.

As a balance to all this machismo, French brand Nickel takes a more jocular approach. Launched by the entrepreneur Philippe Dumont in 1996, the brand was one of the first to establish a 'men only' beauty institute, in the Marais quarter of Paris, with a successful concession opening soon afterwards in the Printemps department store. Its products include Smooth Operator shaving gel, Fire Insurance aftershave moisturizer, Silicon Valley anti-wrinkle cream, and Morning After revitalizing lotion.

Dumont, whose sales have largely relied on highly visible blue packaging, media coverage and word of mouth, says that he targets men directly – without trying to seduce their partners first. 'I figure [men] are big enough to take care of themselves,' he told the Canadian website Amabilia.com in 2006. In the same interview, he admitted that most men did not regard skincare as essential. 'Fundamentally, a man could go his entire life without using a single cosmetic product,' he said. 'The generations before us did so. So it's not a case of necessity, it's a case of, "Is it fun, am I more at ease, does it make me feel good?" We don't need to talk about men's "problems". But we can say that it's probably better to arrive at work in the morning without anybody being able to tell that you've been partying all night.'

Another French male skincare brand, Skeen+, has a sombre, scientific air. Its Paris store resembles a library, with no-nonsense, colour-coded products neatly aligned on shelves like the spines of books. A lone computer on a pedestal at the back of the long, uncluttered space reinforces the feeling that this is a centre of expertise, where men's skin will, quite literally, be in safe hands. The store may have a Scandinavian sparseness about it, but its owner is exotically Latin: born in Uruguay to an Italian family, Pedro Garcia Maggi attended a French school in Montevideo before arriving in Paris 15 years ago to study human resources. After an internship at L'Oréal, he was hired to work in the company's marketing department. Eventually he was made marketing direc-tor of the Vichy brand, which was being re-positioned. 'They wanted to turn it into a medically-oriented skincare product,' he recalls. 'So I travelled throughout Europe, the United States and Asia, talking to dermatologists and researching the evolution of the sector. I learned that the health of our skin is governed by only a few effective molecules. Therefore the number of active ingredients in any skincare product is limited. All the rest is just marketing. In fact, as the industry survives on volume sales, very few branded skincare products contain the pure ingredients used by dermatologists.'

Armed with this knowledge, Maggi decided to leave L'Oréal and create his own range of skincare products based on dermatological research. His multi-functional 12-product anti-ageing line is designed to be as effective as a pharmacy brand. 'I mobilized a team of dermatologists, biochemists and pharmacists to come up with a radical anti-aging formula for men, using pure ingredients with genuine dermatological benefits.'

He briskly dismisses this idea that men are becoming 'feminized' in their approach to skincare. 'There are a lot of myths about the male skincare market. In fact, for years men have wanted exactly the same as women: products that are simple, effective and based on research.'

Although Skeen+ is located in the Marais quarter of Paris – an area known for its sizeable gay community – Maggi denies that gay consumers are his primary target market. 'My products are for intelligent men looking for products that they can trust. My aim is to take a more sophisticated approach to male skincare. When you look at men's products from major brands, they have an extremely patronizing marketing proposition. It's always about sport, outdoors, virility, freshness and so on. Does anybody still buy into that?'

The 'anti-packaging' packaging of the products – with simple descriptions apparently typewritten on brightly-coloured labels – came about almost by chance. 'We used the same system during clinical tests, so the laboratory didn't get the different samples mixed up. In the end I got used to it, so I asked our designer to adopt the same style.'

An unusual feature of the L-shaped store is a small gallery space for local artists. Combined with the soothing ambient music, it adds to the intelligent yet cocooning atmosphere. 'I wanted it to be a place where people could come and seek advice, and maybe stay for a while,' says Maggi. 'It should be a relaxing experience, which sits easily with notions of health and well-being.'

Less surprisingly, a qualified dermatologist is on hand to analyse the client's skin using two hand-held scanners. Users see their skin magnified several thousand times on the computer screen and hear about sun damage, hydration and elasticity. 'The analytical aspect really appeals to our customers, who are surprisingly knowledgeable about dermatology even before they walk in the door,' says Maggi. 'Once they learn about what's going on with their skin, they rarely leave with just one product.'

The minimalist packaging of Skeen+ products bears a passing resemblance to that of Kiehl's. Today owned by L'Oréal, the venerable shaving and skincare brand claims to have been founded as an 'old world apothecary' in the East Village of New York in 1851. The original store certainly looks authentic enough. The brand plays on a classic barbershop aesthetic, leavened with irony, through products like its 'Close Shavers' Squadron' cream, 'Facial Fuel' moisturizer and 'Ultimate Man' body scrub soap. Although it also provides products for women – as well as babies and even pets – its heritage, no-nonsense labelling and gentle humour combine to deliver a high comfort factor for male consumers.

Perhaps in a bid to add a bit of derring-do into the mix, Kiehl's claims that a 1988 Mount Everest expedition team took a selection of the brand's products on the climb with them. While lip balm and moisturizer are undoubtedly essential when you're scaling the side of a mountain, it seems harder to believe that the climbers had recourse to the 'Cucumber Herbal Alcohol-free Toner' or the 'Imperiale Repaireateur Moisturizing Masque' – both of which feature in the 'Everest 88 Collection'. But if it helps us all feel a little more intrepid while we're pampering ourselves, let's just go along with the idea.

MALE BEAUTY PARLOURS

Among the places where men feel most comfortable, beauty insti-
tutes and health spas are hardly at the top of the list. That was
certainly the feeling of Laith Waines before he became co-founder
and managing director of The Refinery, an expanding chain of
'men's grooming emporia' that also has a line of skincare products.
A former investment banker, Waines admits that throughout his
twenties, his grooming routine 'basically involved soap and the
occasional dip into my girlfriend's moisturizer'.

All that changed when he began dating a woman who was seriously into health spas, and who encouraged him to join her. 'I
found myself getting massages and facials, which I would never
have done before. While these experiences were highly agreeable,
the clientele was 95 per cent female, and I felt very self-conscious
trailing around the spa in my towelling robe. But the germ of
the idea was there: I thought that if I could provide a masculine
version of this service, I might be on to something.'

When Waines quit banking in 1998, he teamed up with a friend to
bring his idea to life. 'We felt that if we were going to do this, it
had to be done properly. It had to be a high-end experience.'

So the pair found a Georgian townhouse in London's Brook
Street, opposite Claridge's Hotel. This was the heart of Mayfair
– a district that has been linked with male elegance ever since
Regency dandy George 'Beau' Brummell strode the streets in his
immaculate white necktie and champagne-polished boots. The
building itself already had a clubby, restrained atmosphere, which
Waines and his colleagues drew on while designing their brand.
The 3,500-square-metre space is distributed over a number of
floors, giving an impression of privacy. There are nine treatment
rooms, along with a barbering salon and a lounge. Colours are
soothing and neutral: white, grey, charcoal, mahogany, beige...
The 'therapists' are attractive women.

The Refinery is also notable for its discretion. It feels like a hermetic universe, screened from the street. While women's nail salons often feature giant windows, the last thing a man wants when he's getting a manicure is to be on display to passers-by. When it comes to their looks, men are hypocrites.

'Every aspect had to be carefully planned, right down to the language on the treatment menu,' says Waines. 'We knew straight away that we had to steer clear of anything that shouted "beauty" and focus very much on "grooming". We also felt that men would be more comfortable taking advice on how to improve their appearance from women.'

Working on the logic that men's priorities are a decent haircut and a shave, The Refinery at first leaned heavily on its barbering to generate loyalty. 'But even then, we knew we had to offer a remarkable experience. Few men see the point of a fifty quid haircut. So we provide a consultation service, a scalp massage, a precision cut from a top stylist, and a hot towel at the end. Our traditional wet shave is equally luxurious.'

The strategy of pitching men with a few extras while they're in the barber's chair is as old as the question 'Something for the weekend, sir?', and it shows no sign of dying out. In the United States, the brand Aveda (owned by the ever-pioneering Estée Lauder) launched its first male grooming collection by sending 85,000 product samples to 6,000 hair salons around the country. These came 'complete with a detailed guide suggesting language, dress code and marketing strategies design to make men feel more comfortable when reaching for premium shampoo'. ('Beauty companies sniff out men's grooming sales', *Brandweek*, 9 July 2007.)

To smooth the way from a haircut and a shave to a less familiar treatment, The Refinery introduced the concept of 'The Pit Stop'. 'It was a way of suggesting a 15-minute manicure, pedicure or massage in the kind of language a guy can deal with. The idea was that he'd come in for a haircut but hang around for a few extra minutes for a manicure.'

Waines says he relies on word of mouth and media coverage to attract customers. Crucially, he also depends on women. 'One of the things that surprised me the most when we opened was the number of men who turned up at the urging of their women. A large proportion of our new business is driven by gift vouchers, and most of those are bought by women for Father's Day or birthdays.'

An early illustration of the influence of women was provided before the emporium had even opened. A delay in the refurbishment process meant that instead of welcoming its first customers in November 1999, as had originally been planned, The Refinery did not open for business until January 2000. In the meantime, though, *The Sunday Times Style* magazine had run a double-page article about the project. This meant that by the time The Refinery was actually up and running, it had already sold £20,000 worth of gift vouchers – mostly to women. 'They were picking their way through what was practically a building site to buy vouchers,' Waines recalls.

This echoes a comment by Wholeman's Bob Ager, who notes that many of the customers buying lotions and potions in his store are women. Waines accepts that women will always 'want their man to look good', but he believes that men have become bolder in the few years since he founded his business. 'Today, our clients regard The Refinery as a lifestyle brand along the same lines as Armani. Being a regular customer is something you can be proud of – it's part of your self-image. The workplace is competitive and you need to look your best. A bar of soap isn't good enough any more.'

The company now has three emporia in London (having taken over the running of the barbershop at Harrods) and an outlet in Tokyo.

In 2004 it launched its line of skincare products in association with Aromatherapy.

While The Refinery was something of a pioneer, it is not alone. Male spas have been springing up for a while now. In the United States, they are usually more blatantly testosterone-driven offerings, with beer and TV sports on offer while a barber goes about his business. One of the models Waines looked at while planning his project was John Allan's, the New York grooming establishment founded way back in 1988. Owner John Allan Meing currently has four salons in New York. And although the atmosphere feels classically American, Meing trained with top chopper Jean Louis David in Paris, where he learned that getting a haircut could be a luxurious experience. Now, for US$65 or an annual fee of US$600 for unlimited visits, clients of John Allan's can get cuts ranging from a straightforward trim to an hour-long treatment – once again including a scalp massage and a hot towel – as well as a manicure, a shoeshine and a beer. Indeed, the bar and pool table contribute to the clubby, 'rat pack' ambience.

'It doesn't matter who you are – when you're sitting in our chairs, we're going to treat you like the most important person in the world,' John Allan Meing told *The New York Times*. 'As a guy, when you feel good about grooming, the whole process stops becoming a chore and starts becoming part of your usual routine.' ('Where guys can indulge in a little "me" time', *The New York Times*, 16 April 2007.)

John Allan's is essentially a barber shop with side orders, but as he observed in another interview, this time with ABC Eyewitness News, 'When I started in 1988, a manicure was like a root canal.' ('The spa treatment… for men', 17 March 2007.) Today, though, 'along with the gym, the car, the relationship, the diet, all of that, we're the last spoke of that wheel'.

There is still room for expansion in the men's skincare market. But the very nature of the male consumer is likely to place a cap on growth. While women often treat skincare and cosmetics as a pleasurable indulgence, shopping for these products as enthusiastically as they do for clothing, men need a concrete reason to buy a product. For them, everything relates back to function.

BRANDING TOOLKIT

- Never underestimate the influence of women.

- Address fears of ageing.

- Link skincare products to the shaving ritual.

- Borrow the language of sports and science: stress functionality.

- Choose *authentic* male role models.

- A hint of retro luxury appeals: think traditional barbershop.

- Self-deprecating humour can work.

- The internet is an ideal environment for reaching men.

- Men are highly discreet in matters of personal care.

- Department stores should cater for men with specific sections and evening shopping events.

2

Cloth

Scene Two: The Bedroom

His charcoal wool Hugo Boss suit is hanging on the wardrobe door. He thinks of himself as the kind of man who might one day have a tailor, but for the moment that remains an idle fantasy. Instead he sticks to a limited range of trusted brands: Boss, Dunhill, Paul Smith, Thomas Pink… For weekends there is Gap, Polo, Hackett and Levi's; for underwear there is Calvin Klein, D&G and good old Marks & Spencer. He is well-dressed, in a conservative way. Like most men, he is risk-averse when it comes to fashion. Aside from the occasional frivolity, he aims for quality and value for money. Although he appreciates the concept of shopping as a leisure activity, his own excursions tend to be brief and purposeful. His goal, if you asked him, is to look 'smart' – although he'd have difficulty defining exactly what that means.

He straightens the knot of the dark blue silk tie (Lanvin: a gift) at the neck of the pale blue Thomas Pink shirt. Today he has decided to wear the Dunhill silver cufflinks in the shape of steering wheels – he likes this touch of boyish humour. The black Samsonite PRO-DLX bag he needs for his Paris trip is already packed: lightweight, discreet, with wheels and a retractable handle. He takes his Tag Heuer Carrera Automatic from the pool of light on the bedside table and snaps its steel bracelet onto his wrist with a satisfying click. It is not yet 7.30am, and his still-sleeping girlfriend stirs and mumbles as he bends and kisses her neck. They have been together for almost six months now, and she stays over several nights a week, but she shows no sign of giving up her own flat in North London. He's in no hurry – his last relationship ended messily when he admitted that he was not ready to settle down and have kids. He reckons he can hold out for another year or so.

He sits on the end of the bed to tie his Church's shoes, yawns, and stands up to move into the kitchen.

FEAR AND CLOTHING

The mainstream male is almost as averse to shopping for clothes as he is to buying skincare products. According to researcher Mintel, almost three quarters of women (73 per cent) enjoy shopping for clothes compared with 50 per cent of men. 'Consumer research conducted by Mintel over the years has continuously identified that many men are uninterested in fashion and shopping,' it reports. 'Men over the age of 25 often dislike shopping to such an extent that their partners buy the majority of menswear for them.' (Men's Outerwear, UK, January 2007.)

Although spend on menswear is growing, it is falling as a share of overall fashion sales. In the UK, for example, the menswear market grew by 13 per cent to £9 billion between 2001 and 2006, while spend on womenswear increased by 20 per cent. Men have 40 per cent fewer shops devoted to them than women.

The situation may not be as bleak as it appears, however. As men's approach to grooming evolves, they are also becoming more concerned about their attire. They have a renascent interest in cut and colour, and have accepted that dressing well does not denote lack of masculinity. The highest spenders are still younger males, aged 15 to 24, which Mintel calls 'the peacock generation'. In schoolyards, on football stadium terraces, in bars and nightclubs, they are keen to impress, while also making complex statements about tribe and affiliation. But 25 to 35-year-old unmarried or pre-family men in higher income groups are also spending on clothes – a habit that does not necessarily slacken when they have children. The Mintel report refers to a group called 'the fashion unconcerned': men who are interested in looking good without following trends. They are fans of designer brands – because they seek an assurance of quality and a certain prestige. For them, being well-dressed is a way to compete.

For most men over 30, 'well-dressed' does not equate with 'trendy'. In Europe and the United States, designers are returning to tradition. 'When Michael Bastian announced... that he was leaving his post as fashion director at New York's Bergdorf Goodman to design a line of men's clothing, he saw a niche in American menswear no-one else was filling – upscale versions of classic styles,' reported *The Wall Street Journal*. ('Men's aisle gets crowded', 12 December 2006.)

Following the hegemony of 'casual Friday' and the explosion of sportswear in the 1990s, the early years of the 21st century have seen a revival of tailoring. Many younger role models have graduated from the halfway house of wearing a smart jacket with jeans to dressing in suits. This seems to have created a dovetail effect, with a narrowing of the gap between the sartorial styles of two generations. It was not surprising that the singer Bryan Ferry appeared in a *GQ* fashion spread with his two equally well-suited sons ('True Brit', July 2007).

Ferry was also recruited by Burberry for its print advertising, which targeted this new breed of trend-averse yet style-aware older man. Mintel goes so far as to suggest that fashion brands are missing out on an untapped market of mature male shoppers, who have money to spend but find that their needs aren't catered for. Products and retail environments tend to be focused on the young, the assumption being that older consumers will adapt. But there is a new breed of shopper who does not want to resemble his father, while requiring a more sophisticated approach than his son. A sober retail space, an honest price–quality rapport and knowledgeable service are all keys here. Brands that are perceived to have achieved this combination are rewarded with fierce loyalty: Hugo Boss, Ralph Lauren and Giorgio Armani are typical examples. In his usual contradictory manner, man is often less fussy about price once he has become hooked on a brand.

Brand loyalty may drive the creation of internet shopping sites for men – an area that still has untapped potential. Although women's sites like Net-a-Porter have been hugely successful, there are few spaces on the web devoted purely to men's fashion. Consistently ahead of the pack in his understanding of the male market, Ralph Lauren has launched Polo.com, which includes a 'style guide' for men. And London-based entrepreneur Ali Khan is going the multi-brand route with Men à la Mode (www.menalamode.com), which offers brands such as Paul & Joe, Holland Esquire, Nicole Farhi and Ungaro. The *Financial Times* commented: 'Prices don't go north of £1,000 and the silhouettes aren't challenging' ('Why online fashion hasn't clicked for men', 19 May 2007). Khan pointed out that almost every other sector is 'light years ahead' of men's fashion when it comes to online retail. But the *FT* cautioned that men have a threshold when it comes to spending online: 'A suit for £3,000-plus is an in-person purchase.' For many men, the cap is much lower.

But the Western male is also becoming richer. There are now more millionaires than ever before, with the number rising by 8.6 per cent in 2006, according to *The Wall Street Journal*'s Wealth Report (27 June 2007). The population of 'high net worth' individuals is growing, creating a new generation of male luxury brand consumers.

Characteristically on-trend, the designer Tom Ford is surfing the Zeitgeist as far as men and shopping are concerned. Ford, of course, transformed the fortunes of the Gucci brand. Hard though it might be to believe now, there was a time when Gucci was regarded as an outmoded maker of soft brown bags and flashy footwear for the sun-dried jet set. During Ford's ten years as creative director of the group, Gucci's image became young, sleek, coruscating and sexy, and its sales increased from US$230 million in 1994 to almost US$3 billion in 2003. Although he was a graduate of the Parsons School of Design, it is accepted that the magic dust he sprinkled over Gucci contained as much marketing savvy as it did fashion design skill.

Following his departure from the Gucci Group in 2004, Ford has been honing his own brand. After forays into eyewear and fragrances, he surprisingly turned his back on womenswear to create an upmarket Tom Ford menswear and accessory collection. His first boutique opened at 845 Madison Avenue in spring 2007. The sumptuous dual-level space – which resembles a luxury hotel room crossed with a gentlemen's club – features US$3,000 ready-to-wear suits downstairs, with a tailoring service upstairs (accessible by mahogany staircase or velvet-lined elevator). But that is to understate the scale of Ford's ambition, as he aims to provide an entire impeccable universe where the wealthy man-about-town can feel at home as he selects suits, shirts, dressing gowns, colognes, luggage and footwear – largely made to his own specifications. On his website, Ford states: 'It should feel as if old Hollywood invented a men's couture salon.'

New York magazine pointed out that Ford's store was located in what it called a 'neo-traditional menswear nexus', alongside brands such as Ralph Lauren, Penhaligon's (old-fashioned toiletries) and Silvano Lattanzi (handmade Italian shoes). It continued: 'As business-casual fades and runway fashion gets ever spookier, another generation of businessmen and stylish dressers is turning to tailored clothing, barbershop shaves, and hand-stitched monograms.' ('Tom Ford opens on Madison Avenue', 23 April 2007.)

Could this be the return of the dandy?

THE REPRESSION OF MENSWEAR

A couple of exhibitions in recent years have drawn attention to the societal pressures that contorted men's approach to clothing – and to dressing – with the result that one of the signifiers of mature masculinity became a lack of interest in fashion. In late 2005, the fashion wing of the Louvre in Paris – the Musée de la Mode – staged an exhibition called *L'Homme Paré*, or 'The Adorned Male'. Then in the autumn of 2006 The New York Public Library was the setting for a show called A Rakish History of Men's Wear. Both exhibitions agreed that sartorial negligence is a fairly recent phenomenon: for many hundreds of years, men cared very much about the way they dressed.

Paula A. Baxter, the curator of the New York exhibition, observes that man initially dressed to indicate his place in society. Garments signified wealth, rank or responsibility. Such was the importance of clothing that dress codes were regulated by sumptuary laws at various points in history. Under the Roman Empire, in the Japan of the Shoguns, in the English Middle Ages and in Renaissance Europe, laws were established to ensure that only the powerful and privileged could flaunt ostentatious attire. Occasionally these rules were introduced to limit spending on scarce products and imported textiles; more often they contrived to put people in their place. For example, members of the emerging French merchant class – the bourgeoisie – of the late 13th century were detested by the aristocracy for their extravagant tastes and fine clothing, which put their supposed betters to shame. In his superb book *Paris: A Secret History* (2006), Andrew Hussey explains: 'It was dislike and fear of [the] emergent middle classes which best explains the bizarre new laws set up by Philippe le Bel (the "Fair") in 1294 that forbade any bourgeois from owning a carriage, wearing ermine or precious stones, or owning more than one set of robes per year, and decreed that they had to limit themselves to locally grown food. The laws were quickly ignored and commercial Paris flourished as wine-makers, spice merchants, tailors and jewellers flocked to Paris from all over Europe to meet the ever-growing demands of its wealthy merchant classes.' Flash, it seems, will out.

As Paula Baxter explains, menswear has also been closely linked to the military. 'The earliest ideals of manhood were based on the warrior, who chose adornment that manifested his overt masculinity and bravery… Garments for combat were generally intended to be colourful, decorative, and functional.' ('A Rakish History of Men's Wear', exhibition guide, September 2006.)

The emergence of tailoring is directly linked to the evolution of the uniform, with its notions of disciplined cut and proportion, while early examples of 'fashionable' menswear take their cue from horsemanship and other martial skills. But if male dress has from the very beginning been codified and regulated, it has also been consistently subverted by rakish outsiders. 'A universal truth emerged early on,' Baxter writes. 'Young men are quick to adopt flashy, often sexually provocative garments as a means of advertising their virility.' Outré stylishness, she adds, acts as 'a goad to dress norms'.

A shadowy reflection of this sensibility can be seen among British football fans. As the style writer Robert Elms underlines in his sartorial memoir *The Way We Wore* (2005), British male fashion has for the last 50 years been built from the bottom up, by working class lads on the streets. Tracing the history of his own fashion enthusiasms, Elms takes us from mod to skinhead, from disco to punk and on to the experiments of the New Romantics in the eighties – and beyond. But he never neglects the influence of the terraces. 'There's always been a close relationship between football and fashion. The terraces, when there were terraces, were the perfect theatre of display, and the most immediate means of communicating new trends. The skinhead look, for example, emerged from mod via the West Ham mob, and in the one season, 1968–9, spread around the country. I can still vividly recall being taken to Chelsea as a ten- or eleven-year-old and seeing a guy standing at their end in a canary yellow Harrington [jacket], and being told he was the leader of the Shed.'

He returns to the theme in the 1980s, when the 'Casuals' emerged, rigged out in their bizarre melange of European sportswear and British golfing attire: Fiorrucci jeans meet a Lacoste shirt under a Pringle sweater, or thereabouts. Accessories included a Stanley knife in the back pocket. More recently, the emerging British menswear designer Aitor Throup showed, in September 2006, a collection that combined military influences with 'hooligan wear'. Born in Argentina but raised in the northern town of Burnley, Throup was inspired by a stint working as a sales assistant for casual clothing brand CP Company. He told *i-D* magazine: 'It was during the time when labels like CP and Stone Island were key labels for football hooligans. I was never one of them but I wore their gear.' ('Aitor Throup – Football gets fashionable', September 2006.)

But while Mintel's 'peacock generation' ruffle their plumage in tribal display on the terraces, the older man remains buttoned up in his sober charcoal suit. What horrible upheaval convinced the mature Western male that he should subdue, truss and pluck his inner peacock? According to the exhibition *L'Homme Paré*, the French Revolution is to blame.

The birth of men's fashion in France took place under the reign of Louis XIV, who established the royal court at Versailles in 1682. Marked by an attempted uprising during his youth, he was determined to keep his closest advisors – and his potential enemies – close to him. So both king and courtier lived in the countryside at Versailles, away from dangerous external influences and assassination plots. The king dressed extravagantly and his courtiers, who were forever at close quarters, had no choice but to do the same. In fact, they competed with one another to see who could wear the most audacious costumes: richly decorated capes, sleeves garnished with ribbon or lace and clothes of satin or velvet, depending on the season.

By the early 18th century, complex garments such as *haut-de-chausses* (breeches) and the *pourpoint* (doublet), and the capes that covered them, had evolved into a simpler three-piece outfit – an early version of the contemporary suit. But although lines had been pared down, men lost none of their peacock tendencies: coats featured complex embroidery and highly decorative buttons in silver, copper, pearl or gold. Buttons were also painted with coloured varnishes or ornamented with complex filigree patterns.

The 18th century male was even more of a bird of paradise in private. Casual silk robes with voluminous sleeves, worn while relaxing at home (the distant cousin of the smoking jacket), were inspired by the Orient, particularly Persia, and featured glorious symmetrical floral patterns. These baroque designs found their way into daytime wear in the form of extravagant waistcoats. New weaving methods made such garments easier to produce and thus more affordable. Today, while waistcoats come and go, the tie remains the only constant outlet for men's baroque fantasies.

The revolution of 1789 and its aftermath put an end to the French male's strutting. Dressing ostentatiously had been, after all, the habit of the aristocracy. Once heads had rolled, clothing became democratized: plain and streamlined, with only vertical stripes to provide visual interest. French men adopted English dress habits, which had always been more practical because English aristocrats were traditionally landowners, rather than courtiers, and prized simple, resilient, practical clothes for riding.

In the Napoleonic era, only the military were allowed overtly colourful costumes, and both soldiers and emperors wore their dashing uniforms for social occasions. After the restoration and into the Second Empire, the black frock coat or *redingote* (a corruption of the English 'riding coat'), worn with a plain black waistcoat and trousers, became the uniform of the elegant man about town. Many fashionable males approved of this sharp black look. The poet Baudelaire considered that, 'the greatest colourists know how to make colour with a black suit, a white tie, and a grey waistcoat'. He also felt that black had 'not only a political beauty, as the expression of universal elegance, but also a poetic beauty. We are all celebrating the death of something'.

Similar views had been expounded several decades earlier, on the other side of the Channel, by a man whose influence lingers over British male dress to this day: George 'Beau' Brummell, the first of the dandies.

Born on 7 June 1778 into a rather *arriviste* upper-middle-class family with political connections, Brummell became a friend of the Prince Regent and the ultimate male icon of his day. He was what all men seem eternally to require when it comes to matters of style: a role model. A pupil at Eton and then a soldier with the 'Prince's Own' regiment – the 10th Regiment of Light Dragoons – Brummell synthesized schoolboy and military influences, together with the pared-down English equestrian style favoured by French revolutionaries, into an outfit of brutal simplicity. If your clothing provoked raised eyebrows – or even a sideways glance – you were overdressed, in Brummell's opinion. What he sought was not ostentation, but perfection.

The basic Brummell look can be summarized as follows: a snowy white shirt and cravat (or 'neckcloth') under a pale or white waistcoat; form-fitting white or buff breeches or pantaloons, either in a woven stocking material or in soft leather, secured by braces; a dark blue jacket with tails, adorned with brass buttons and sculpted by the tailor to suggest an athletic physique; black Hessian riding boots.

After the lacy and embroidered fopperies that had preceded it, this ruthlessly streamlined look was a fashion electroshock. As Ian Kelly puts it in his (2005) biography *Beau Brummell: The Ultimate Dandy*, 'it was the ideal visual corollary of Empire: noble, muscular, self-evidently aspirational, utterly uneffeminate'. And although it might seem severe today, at the time the ensemble spoke of liberty and physicality. The clothes were 'the casual sportswear of their day – Hessian riding boots, riding breeches and cutaway riding jackets – so that even West End "loungers", who had no intention of riding anywhere, could give the appearance of readiness to mount a horse and gallop towards revolution'. Suitably enough, much of Brummell's socializing was done at the theatre, whose stalls played the role that the football terraces would a couple of centuries later.

As one might expect given his high public profile, Brummell was sought out for early forms of celebrity endorsement. The (1999) book *The Hidden Consumer*, by Christopher Breward, offers an interesting insight into Brummell's relationship with the tailor Stultz, via a clipping from an 1872 edition of the magazine *The Tailor and Cutter*. 'Stultz… conceived the idea of making a coat for Brummell… The coat was sent with a £100 note in the pocket. Brummell acknowledged the receipt of the coat, adding that the lining was very acceptable. An arrangement was made whereby Stultz sent Brummell a new coat in a new style at the beginning of each month, each having a £100 note in the pocket… '

Such was Brummell's influence that a coterie of admiring men – which included the Prince Regent – would call by his rooms in the morning to watch him dress. Nobody had such skill with a necktie, it seems. He also introduced elements of male grooming that are familiar to us today, but were unusual for the era. For instance, Kelly tells us that he 'exfoliated his body all over with a coarse horse-hair brush'. He also bathed and changed his clothes several times a day. Of course, the immaculately white shirtfronts and cravats sported by Brummell and his followers also signified status – only wealthy young men could afford such a quantity of freshly laundered material. Those dashing jackets, too, demanded a high level of craftsmanship if they were to transform a well-fed London dandy into a broad-shouldered yet sleek Adonis. 'The real art of bespoke tailoring,' Kelly writes, 'was born from this need to define each body according to a perceived ideal, rather than swathe a body generically in fabric suited to his class.'

An armature of tailoring over a smart shirt and necktie: Brummell's legacy, then, was the ubiquitous suit.

THE IMPORTANCE OF BEING SUITED

Though Brummell had chased overt fantasy from the male wardrobe, men did not entirely renounce an interest in fashion – even if they felt compelled to feign unconcern. In *The Hidden Consumer*, Christopher Breward rejects the theory of 'The Great Masculine Renunciation', usually sited at the end of the 18th century. '[This] has provided... a convenient shorthand for a stylistic progression of cut and colour that is undoubtedly rather limiting and impenetrable when compared to the wilder fluctuations of female dress at the time,' he writes. But he argues that notions of 'elaboration' and 'elegance' in the masculine wardrobe survived, to be promoted by the clothing industry and 'eagerly consumed' by men.

He concedes that obvious finery and foppishness were killed off by the emergence of ready-to-wear, thanks to 'mechanization via the sewing machine in the late 1860s'. Demand for more clothing, faster, led to the simplification of the suit. Mass production meant that male clothing in the late 19th century was marked by 'the comfort of a tubular looseness and a subdued conformity of colour and texture'.

But it should not be inferred that men lost their sense of style. Breward offers this quote from an 1872 book called *Fashion: The Power that Influences the World*, by G.P. Fox: 'It is universally admitted that nothing marks the gentleman more than the style of his dress. The elegance, propriety and good taste which are conspicuous in that, at once create a presumption in his favour.' Or, to borrow a line from the impeccable Oscar Wilde, 'It is only shallow people who do not judge by appearances.'

Breward also notes that the 19th-century male consumer was, as ever, a target for marketing material. Handbills circulated at the Great Exhibition of 1851 in London promoted the house of N. Benjamin (at 78 Westminster Bridge Road): 'The cheapest tailoring and outfitting establishment in the world!' Advertisements at the time used a bizarre stew of slang derived from the military, the music hall and the streets. One C. Greenburg, 'the noted working men's tailor', claimed to be 'the only genuine clothing manufacturer in Chelsea for flash toggery'. Another retailer on the Westminster Bridge Road, Charles Lyons, ran a rhyming advertising campaign: 'The wool dyed black suit, at two pounds and ten / Is a fact seen every now and then. / But at C. Lyons, near the railway / It may be seen at any hour of the day.'

This colourful language, suggests Breward, works against the theory that men 'somehow resisted the blandishments of consumer culture through an adherence to rational decision-making pro-cesses' and that 'any enthusiasm for or fetishizing of the product were peculiar to the feminine environment of the department store'.

In fact, menswear stores were being overhauled at the tail end of the 19th century. Before mass production, tailors had been purely functional spaces – often located on the upper floors of buildings housing multifarious activities – so there was no need for shop windows or attractive interior design. But as the industrial revo-lution took hold and the consumer society emerged, so did eye-catching window displays and comfortable interiors. For men's retailers, as Breward points out, this meant balancing the 'feminized' visual attractiveness of the department store with the more rational shopping approach of the male consumer. A display devoted to tweed, for example, might depict every stage of the production process: a stuffed sheep, a loom, samples of cloth, the tailor's sketches, and finally a mannequin clad in the finished garment. All this spoke of authenticity, rigour, and quality. And as cutters and tailors began to disappear, store displays incorporated ghostly reminders of their presence via 'virgin bales of textile awaiting the attention of the absent craftsman's shears and fashion plate templates suggestive of suits to come'.

With the emergence of ready-to-wear, tailoring slowly became the province of the elite. And yet the ideal of remaining loyal to a trusted outfitter remained lodged in the DNA of male consumers; as did the need for attentive service. The interiors of many contemporary menswear stores contain faint echoes of the descriptions above. The outlets of the designer Paul Smith, for example, with their wood cabinets and collections of curios, provide distinctly masculine environments that answer several male needs: the sense of worldliness, the obsession with gadgets, a certain irony, a hint of schoolboy whimsy – and the old-world classicism of a traditional tailor.

Of course, the real thing is still available – at a price. The heartland of traditional tailoring is undoubtedly London's Savile Row. So vital is this single street to the history of men's suiting that the Japanese word for suit is *'seiburo'* – a corruption of the words 'Savile Row'. Although tailors and boot-makers had clustered in the streets around The Row during the early 19th century, the first tailor to open for business there was Henry Poole, in 1846. Lately there have been signs that The Row is being nibbled away at the edges; the arrival of a branch of US casualwear brand Abercrombie & Fitch ('Nothing but an oversexed Gap', sniffed one tailor) caused consternation in some quarters.

Happily, though, the future of Savile Row seems assured. In 2004, Mark Henderson – managing director of Gieves & Hawkes, based at Number One Savile Row – formed an alliance with four other tailors to create an association called Savile Row Bespoke. Its mission is to protect and promote the art of bespoke tailoring on The Row. The founder members, along with Gieves & Hawkes, were Henry Poole, Anderson & Sheppard, Huntsman and Dege & Skinner. 'They were all companies with over 100 years of experience in providing a bespoke service from their own workshops,' says Henderson. Today, the association embraces

14 tailoring firms, including youthful newcomers like Ozwald Boateng and Richard James. Savile Row Bespoke became a registered trademark in 2006 and the group is supported by Westminster City Council, which has pledged to protect around 20,000 square feet of workroom space. The Row is still home to more than 100 tailors, who proudly claim to train longer than doctors. Henderson, chairman of Savile Row Bespoke, believes the brand is as important to England as Champagne is to France.

'Fortunately,' he says, 'fashion seems to be on our side. The height of the dotcom boom was a terribly difficult time, when suits were definitely "out" among younger men. This did have the positive effect, however, of ridding men of the cheap suit as work uniform. Today there's a great deal of interest in bespoke tailoring, with designers like Tom Ford and Armani offering bespoke services. It's now a luxury lifestyle option rather than some arcane craft.'

The figures bear him out. According to an article in the *Financial Times*, 'Savile Row has rarely been in better shape, turning over an annual £21m collectively for the bespoke service... Everyone from Tom Ford to Jude Law shops there, not to mention the crowned heads, politicians and captains of industry who have been patronizing The Row for two centuries, as well as an estimated 10,000 others'. ('Bespoke bites back', 1 April 2006.)

'Bespoke' should not be confused with 'made-to-measure'. A bespoke suit is made from scratch to your ('spoken') specifications and exact measurements, while a made-to-measure suit is customized to fit you from an existing model. As the *Financial Times* article observed, a bespoke Savile Row suit does not come cheap, but for between £2,000 and £3,000 you can have a 'little piece of English heritage', while 'a Brioni suit with a chinchilla collar is about £20,000 and an Alexander McQueen leather jacket £6,000'.

Giorgio Armani was less than kind about Savile Row when he launched his own bespoke service, describing British tailoring as 'a melodrama lost in the past'. He added: 'They don't research or develop something or innovate. There is no room in their head to expand into something new... Younger clients want a made-to-measure suit but they are not so keen on all the old traditions.' ('Armani attacks Savile Row', *The Sunday Times*, 9 July 2006.)

In fact, the denizens of The Row have been striving to balance modernity with tradition for some time. Gieves & Hawkes is a good example of a traditional tailor that has managed to dust itself off for a contemporary public. The company dates back to 1785, when Gieves was a naval tailor based in Portsmouth. Hawkes, meanwhile, was a London cap-maker and provider of military attire. The two did not actually merge until 1974, although they had many factors in common: strong links with the armed forces, a succession of royal warrants and 'almost eccentric levels of service,' in the words of Mark Henderson. He provides an example from the Crimean war, when a signal was sent to the Malta branch of Gieves requesting a collar stud. The firm's local manager hired a boat to deliver the item to the customer's ship.

Gieves moved to its current prestigious address – formerly the headquarters of the Royal Geographical Society – in 1912. Its first ready-to-wear collection appeared in 1922. 'The roots of the business are in the services,' says Henderson. 'As well as making uniforms, we made the clothes that military men wore in civilian life. In the sixties and seventies, many of them became City people. They instinctively trusted us because of our military heritage and the sense of gravitas around the name.'

The Gieves & Hawkes brand expanded, opening stores and concessions around the world. But its image remained British, snooty, and middle-aged. That was until 1998, when Gieves & Hawkes launched a second, more fashionable line that would simply be called 'Gieves'. 'At that stage we were perceived as so stuck in our ways that the idea that we could become even the tiniest bit fashionable beggared belief,' chuckles Henderson. 'So we launched Gieves as a capsule collection that sat quietly alongside our traditional offering. But it grew and grew, until finally we decided to show it at [Milan menswear show] Pitti Uomo. We also showed collections in Paris for three seasons.'

The presence of a brand from Savile Row on the catwalks of Milan and Paris was highly unexpected. As a knock-on effect, Gieves & Hawkes sales increased, with younger customers realizing that they appreciated the traditional tailoring as much as the supposedly trendier 'Gieves' garments. For autumn/winter 2007, Gieves and Gieves & Hawkes ready-to-wear collections were shown in Paris side-by-side. 'Our core market is now the 30-plus male with an eye for luxury,' says Henderson. 'In other words, in the past six years the average age of our customer has dropped by more than ten years.'

With this mission accomplished, the 'Gieves' brand was discreetly dropped, and Gieves & Hawkes now stands proudly as a provider of both traditional suiting and younger classics with a twist.

The drawback of a more formal manner of dressing is the sense of discipline that goes along with it. The Brummell-inspired Savile Row tradition is obsessed with 'correctness'. While women have long been liberated from any strict 'rules' of dressing, it appears that men still need a basic template to follow. Men's magazines like *GQ* and *Esquire* are full of tips and quibbles about the 'correct' length of a tie, rise of a trouser, width of a lapel, colour of belt with regards to shoe, and so on. This codified approach to dressing is best illustrated by Alan Flusser's (2002) book, *Dressing the Man: Mastering the Art of Permanent Fashion*. 'Dressing well rests on two pillars – colour and proportion,' he insists. He is nostalgic for the 1930s, 'the last epoch in which a gentleman's ideal was to be attired in "bespoke fashions".' He urges us to study the classic icons of elegance: Fred Astaire, Cary Grant and David Niven. Very few of his role models date from beyond the 1960s. In his defence, Flusser writes: 'Some may feel that establishing rules for good taste may inhibit self-expression. It's my opinion that they provide the only chance for genuine individuality. Real innovation has always taken place with an awareness of, rather than an ignorance of, the rules.'

Even so, the tie around our neck suddenly begins to feel like a noose – one which we may not have tied correctly. It's like punk never happened.

A more recent book called *The Suit*, by Nicholas Antongiavanni (2006), takes a similar stance. '[O]nly men attired in well-balanced, classic silhouettes ever look smart,' its author decrees, before deciding that designer – as opposed to bespoke – suits are 'useless and dangerous; and if one founds his wardrobe on them, he founds on mud, and will never be stylish or even safe'.

The cutting-edge world of the blogosphere is not immune from a preoccupation with correctness. One of the most influential fashion bloggers is The Sartorialist, a New York photographer who takes beautifully-composed shots of people he considers well-dressed and then puts them on his website accompanied by short comments. While his interpretation of style is broad, The Sartorialist (Scott Schuman, who has considerable experience in the fashion industry) occasionally strays into tutorial mode, sketching guidelines of acceptability in dress. At the time of writing, for instance, he has provoked a debate about whether men should wear their trousers at their 'natural' waist, old-school style, or slung low on the hip. Tellingly for our epoch, The Sartorialist, 'one of *Time* magazine's top 100 design influencers', votes old-school.

When the pressure to button up and tone down gets too great, men may turn to the apparently unconventional wardrobes of rock and hip hop. The irony, of course, is that these sartorial universes are as codified as those of Brummell's dandies or of Savile Row. Few men, it seems, are confident enough to dress entirely by instinct.

This need for guidance has marketing implications, because strong role models can exert a powerful influence. When Daniel

Craig became the latest incarnation of James Bond in the film *Casino Royale* (2006), he had an almost immediate impact on the comportment of British males. The Grigio Perla swimming trunks he sported in one scene flew from shelves, despite the fact that they were streamlined European briefs, while British men had typically preferred less risky Bermuda-type beachwear. 'For the first time since the 1970s and early 1980s, the Speedo look, with its higher cut over the hips and figure-hugging contour is back,' reported the *Financial Times*. The article quoted Dan Doyle, menswear buyer at Liberty, who commented: 'In my opinion it's the tight short that conveys real style and is easier for a lot of guys to wear – Daniel Craig in *Casino Royale* springs to mind' ('Briefer encounters', 28 July 2007.) Not only that, but Craig's bulked-up, super-fit look sent men scurrying back to the gym, with subsequent soaring attendance.

RETURN TO CLUBLAND

Although it doesn't actively promote his patronage, menswear and accessories brand Dunhill makes no secret of the fact that Daniel Craig is a customer. But it has other marketing strategies up its well-turned sleeve.

Marketing director Julian Diment describes the brand's target audience as 'successful men aged between 35 and 55', who are 'understated yet individual; fashion-aware without being dictated to by fashion'. These men are discerning, they travel a great deal on business and they tend to be attracted to brands that have a timeless feel about them.

Dunhill's image is that of the quintessentially British male, a character who probably no longer exists but is a powerful and enduring fantasy figure. A template can be found, however, in the form of Alfred Dunhill. In 1893, the 20-year-old Alfred inherited his father Henry's business: a saddler and harness-maker that also provided 'horse clothing of every description'. Unlike his father, who assumed that the new 'horseless carriage' would be a passing fad, Alfred was obsessed by motor cars. He began considering a line of accessories for motorists, despite the fact that by 1895 there were still only a dozen or so automobiles on the roads of Britain. The number quickly swelled, however, and at the end of 1896 the first London to Brighton race took place. Known as the 'Emancipation Run', it was staged to celebrate the scrapping of a law that had limited the speed of motor cars to walking pace. Nick Foulkes writes in the (2005) book *Dunhill by Design* that 'as the horseless carriages put-putted out of London and into the Sussex countryside – often reaching double figures in miles per hour – Alfred Dunhill knew that his fortune was made'.

Dunhill had already doubled the turnover of his business thanks to extensive advertising. Now he identified a new market: 'The name Dunhill, Alfred decided, should become synonymous with the motor car. Motorists, thought the young Dunhill, should have their priorities and he would be the man to supply them.' He launched a range of motoring apparel and accessories called Motorities, with the result that Dunhill became famous for selling 'everything for the car but the motor'.

Motor horns, driving goggles, gloves, timepieces, protective clothing, ('The Siberian Wolf Coat – built from the most carefully matched skins, unequalled for weather-defying qualities'), bespoke luggage and picnic hampers: Dunhill's wide range of products and elegant image reflected the fact that motoring was still the domain of the privileged. The brand has cultivated this air of dashing refinement ever since. Meanwhile, the energetic Alfred was expanding into related areas, offering accessories to motorcyclists and aviators, and launching wind-proof pipes for those who wanted to suck a stem at speed. By the 1920s Dunhill had opened boutiques in Paris and New York. Its range had expanded far beyond motoring accessories and pipes – or even posh lighters – to embrace a wide array of luxury lifestyle products, from fountain pens to cocktail cabinets. The first men's fragrance, Dunhill for Men, was launched in 1934, with a cap that resembled a wheel nut. Inevitably, during the post-war years Dunhill swelled into a global brand. It maintained its prestige across the decades – and even in the taste-free 1970s, Jerry Hall and Bryan Ferry were photographed in its clothing.

Today, says Julian Diment, the brand 'starts and finishes with men'. And its automobile heritage clicks with male customers because, as we've discovered, they appreciate any suggestion of technicality and functionality. 'That's where men and women differ in their psyches. In reality men buy things – even cars – because they look great, but they need to rationalize their decision. So a guy will buy a biker's jacket because he knows he looks good in it, but if you question him on it he'll say he likes the practicality of its hidden pocket.'

Dunhill also draws on the male predilection for gadgets, providing items such as BlackBerry covers and iPod speakers. It has even launched a bag that recharges laptops while their owners are on the move, thanks to a solar panel.

As we've said, Dunhill lets it be known that well-dressed men such as Daniel Craig and Jude Law (who has also featured in its advertising) are among its customers. This tradition dates back to the 1920s, when the Prince of Wales – later Edward VIII and the Duke of Windsor – was a sartorial role-model on both sides of the Atlantic. He would drop in to Dunhill's London flagship at St James's through a side entrance and select a new pipe from the 'Royal Drawer'.

In common with most luxury brands, Dunhill uses print advertising in glossy magazines to promote its products. To underline its brand values and lifestyle positioning, it also engages in sponsorship activities such as the Alfred Dunhill Links Championship – an international golfing event at St Andrews.

But a more recent innovation is perhaps its most ambitious: the creation of Dunhill branded gentlemen's clubs.

'We've identified buildings in London, Shanghai and Tokyo, within which we'll create the ultimate masculine universe,' says Diment. Although there is a retail element to these environments – with tailors and shirt-makers on hand – they will also include barbers, treatment rooms, restaurants, bars, and even bedrooms for those who want to stay overnight. 'The clubs will encompass all the values of the brand: Britishness, quirkiness, and masculinity. They'll be the kind of places that Alfred Dunhill himself might have appreciated, so you'll feel almost as though you're staying in one of his former homes.'

Not unlike Tom Ford, with his clubby emporium, Dunhill is gambling on the fact that today's male seeks an environment in which he can wallow, even for a brief period, in old-fashioned masculinity.

ACCESSORY AFTER THE FACT

Given that they're experimenting with products and even attitudes that were previously associated with women, it comes as no surprise to learn that men are embracing jewellery. Or perhaps we should say 'rediscovering jewellery', as any casual museum visitor knows that men have been adorning themselves for thousands of years. Still within living memory is the 'medallion man' of the 1970s, whose chunky gold talisman nestled in a thicket of chest hair. It was perhaps this derided archetype that sent men scurrying away from adornment during subsequent decades. But now they are edging cautiously back. The heavy 'bling' associated with rappers helped to rescue male jewellery from fashion limbo, and it was not long before it resurfaced in the mainstream. According to the magazine *Modern Jeweller*, the men's sector is 'booming at last'. 'Sure, sales of men's jewellery may be in single digit percentiles for most stores,' the article admits, 'but retailers are reporting noticeable increases'. ('The Men's Boom', June 2007.)

Needless to say, a large percentage of men's jewellery is chosen for them by women – perhaps half of sales, according to *Modern Jeweller*. 'Although everyone agrees that more marketing and advertising of men's lines to men would help everyone, it's important to remember that... the woman consumer is a strong market that must be heeded.' This explains the preponderance of point-of-sale advertising in boutiques and department stores, and the relative paucity of ads for men's jewellery in the male-oriented press.

The return to formal tailoring is driving sales of cuff-links, but less traditional items are also being snapped up: bracelets and dog-tag pendants, for example, as well as rings. Brands such as John Hardy and David Yurman offer jewellery that is subtle and inventive, yet unarguably masculine – such as Yurman's rings and cuff-links featuring exotic stones with fossilized dinosaur bones embedded in them. There's often a hint of the gothic about men's jewellery, which no doubt appeals to the secret rock star in some of us. In general, men like quality rather than 'costume' jewellery; and they respond to inventive blends of materials. The problem is finding the products in the first place, as most jewellers still devote a tiny amount of space to baubles for blokes.

Watches are another story. For years, the watch has been man's only significant accessory. Unable to show off with a handbag, unconvinced that anybody notices his designer suit or leather-soled shoes, and robbed of his sleek automobile by congested urban streets, he communicates his status with a fancy watch. Whether it's Brad Pitt sporting a Tag Heuer, Pierce Brosnan flashing an Omega or Tiger Woods swinging a club in a Rolex, men's publications and jewellery boutiques are cluttered with images of male icons in chunky wrist-wear. A survey of 25,000 UK consumers conducted in 2005 found that 25.8 per cent of men agreed with the statement, 'I often wear a valuable watch,' as opposed to 19.2 per cent of women. The researcher Mintel concluded: 'Leaving aside the fact that inevitably the statement "I often wear a valuable watch" is a highly subjective one, there is a clear difference between men and women. It seems probable that this difference derives directly from the fact that men have fewer means to express their personal style than women.'

The marketing of watches combines some of the most predictable strategies for targeting men: the use of male icons in print advertising, movie product placement (see Chapter 10), and heavy sports sponsorship. There is also an over-emphasis on functionality: men's watches come with an array of functions that their owners will never use, unless they actually *are* a globe-trotting deep-sea diver who dabbles in motor racing and pilots his own aircraft.

But it's important to keep the dream alive.

BRANDING TOOLKIT

■ Stress technical, performance or quality elements.

■ Heritage engenders trust.

■ Confer status.

■ Create loyalty: men are not promiscuous consumers.

■ The retail environment: sober yet relaxed, with impeccable service.

■ Detain the male consumer with additional services, from bookstores to barbershops.

■ Men appreciate guidelines for 'correct' dressing.

■ Retail websites for men have yet to achieve their full potential.

■ Celebrity endorsement and product placement are extremely powerful.

3

Diet

He snaps on the spotlights above his immaculate kitchen. He fancies himself as a bit of a cook, although in reality he often eats out. And now that he's trying to get back into shape for the summer, salads have taken a more prominent place in his diet. Still, the kitchen's gleaming industrial efficiency communicates intent. The stainless steel Delmeyere pans and the Zwilling J.A. Henckels knives are all in place. You could almost walk into the bow-fronted Smeg fridge freezer; and the stocky Neff range looks as if it belongs in the kitchen of a gourmet restaurant.

All this is separated from the living room by a granite-topped counter. When he first looked around the flat, he was pleased to see that the kitchen would be part of his living space. Now his dinner guests can watch him as he dices and sautés and cracks jokes, occasionally cocking his arm to sip from a glass of Shiraz. He's inspired by celebrity chefs like Gordon Ramsay, Tom Aikens and Heston Blumenthal – and the godfather of them all, the incendiary Marco Pierre White, who used to chase critics and philistines out of his restaurants. There's a copy of Marco's book, *White Heat*, sitting on the counter with a pile of other culinary tomes, including recipe books by Nigel Slater and Rick Stein, and

Kitchen Confidential by Anthony Bourdain – another two-fisted chef who reconciled men with ingredients.

There will be no cooking this morning, though. He snaps on a portable radio tuned to BBC London, ears pricked for a traffic report. He pours himself a glass of orange juice, then a bowl of muesli with skimmed milk. For coffee he's finally succumbed to a Nespresso machine, seduced by its convenience and good looks. He sits at the counter dealing with all these and running the day through his head. In less than 15 minutes he will be out of the door.

DIET HARD

In January 2006, a survey revealed that one in three men in the United Kingdom was on a diet. The poll of 2,100 adults by YouGov, an internet-based market research firm, claimed that 39 per cent of men had dieted over the past 12 months, compared with 60 per cent of women. The real figure may be even higher, but men don't like to talk about 'dieting'. They prefer to tell you that they're 'getting into shape', 'getting fit' or 'in training'. 'Language may be only part of what separates the sexes in their attitude to food,' observed *The Times*, 'but it does say that men generally diet for a project, women as a cultural requirement.' ('Fat isn't just a feminine issue', 13 September 2005.)

As with other aspects of contemporary male behaviour, these changing attitudes to diet have been provoked by a combination of factors: the increasing visibility of gay culture; the meshing of sportswear with fashion; and pressure from companies that stand to gain if men become more concerned with their weight. In the same article, Susie Orbach – psychotherapist and the author of the book *Fat is a Feminist Issue* – expressed concern that men were 'buying into' anxiety about what they ate, a problem that had previously been associated with women. She said: 'The point is that many industries stand to profit from this... [such as] the industries that support men's magazines with advertising… [I]t is permeating through from pop culture, this idea of sculpting the male form in sleeker ways.'

Orbach noted that food had been transformed from a fuel to a lifestyle. It is a lifestyle in which men are increasingly encouraged to participate, thanks to the cult of the lovably roguish TV chef. Former soccer player Gordon Ramsay typifies the breed, and a couple of years ago the press slavered over the 'half-million pound kitchen' in his new home, 'whose centrepiece is a £67,000 Rorgue cooker weighing two-and-a-half tonnes'. 'It's about the same size as Gordon's car,' his wife Tana commented, 'and he probably loves it more.' ('The chef, his wife and the £500,000 kitchen', *The Observer*, 15 February 2004.)

Encouraged by women and egged on by the media, men have come to regard cooking as a weapon in their seduction arsenal. A man who knows his way around a kitchen is considered organized and capable, with an attractive streak of sensitivity. And as more men are living alone for longer, a tricked-out kitchen is part and parcel of the 21st-century bachelor pad. In 2007, Porsche Design teamed up with elite German furniture brand Poggenpohl to design a kitchen specifically for male consumers. According to the press release, it would be 'futuristic', 'pure' and – that magic word again – 'functional'.

The branded male's approach to food, then, embraces three concerns: 'eat healthily', 'cook better' and 'look cool while cooking'. The result of this may be overwhelmingly positive, as a varied diet using plenty of fresh ingredients is undoubtedly a wiser one.

In the recent past, there was no social requirement for men to be thin – that pressure was almost entirely borne by women. But brisk sales of magazines like *Men's Health*, as well as 'fitness' books with a male bias, indicate that this is no longer the case. A book called *The Abs Diet* became a bestseller on both sides of the Atlantic in 2005 when it was positioned as 'the first diet book written from a male perspective'. It smartly focused on the Holy Grail of dieting men: a flat stomach. (Men tend to store excess fat around the abdomen, while in women it gathers on hips and thighs.) Interestingly, it was co-written by David Zinczenko, the editor-in-chief of... *Men's Health* magazine.

Launched in the United States in 1986 by Rodale Press, *Men's Health* is now the world's best-selling male lifestyle magazine, with a readership of 18.5 million and 33 editions worldwide, including markets such as India, Korea, Malaysia and the Philippines. While the first issue sold only 90,000 copies, interest in the publication has grown as male attitudes have evolved. The magazine works because it is positioned as a 'tool for better living', and any claims made in its pages are underpinned by the advice of scientists and experts, with statistics backing them up. This package undoubtedly appeals to the man as predator: become leaner, fitter, cooler, and more efficient.

Plenty of other services have sprung up for men who want to eat healthily and sculpt their figures. For example, *The New York Times* reported on overweight male executives who 'jump start' their fitness regimes by enrolling in pricey spas and diet centres. 'There's no question I overeat,' admitted one executive, who said he combated this tendency by paying US$2,250 for a five-day programme at the Duke Diet and Fitness Center in Durham, North Carolina. ('Men join the migration to the halls of diet and fitness', 23 April 2006.) Meanwhile, a spokeswoman from the Pritikin Longevity Center and Spa in Aventura, Florida, confirmed that half her customers were men. These executives – who usually enrolled under their own steam, rather than being goaded by their partners – paid about US$5,000 for a week at the centre. Adopting a military theme common to coverage of men's fitness regimes, the article continued: 'Spending a week at Pritikin [is] more like undergoing boot camp than a spa treatment... The emphasis [is] not on cucumber facials and the other hallmarks of spa frivolity, but on the serious unisex business of physical fitness and sensible eating habits.'

And yet it appears that some men take the same hit-and-run approach to fitness as they do to shopping. The executives in the *New York Times* article felt that the solution to overeating was to visit a fitness centre for an intensive weight-loss treatment 'three or four times a year'. As they struggle to burn fat, they stay in touch with the business world via wireless internet and cell phones.

British men have an equally confused approach to dieting. 'All this sudden incitement to lose the lipids feels like being thrown into an exam without having been taught the syllabus. When my ex-flatmate decided to go on a diet, I came home to find him preparing supper: eight Ryvita covered in butter and cheese.' ('Going belly up', *The Observer*, 24 February 2002.)

This confusion – caused by mixed messages and a lack of well-publicized information from authoritative sources – is potentially dangerous. The (2000) book *Making Weight: Men's Conflicts with Food, Weight, Shape and Appearance* warned of the torture that awaited men who became obsessed with their figures. Jointly written by two doctors and an expert on eating disorders (Arnold Andersen, M.D., Thomas Holbrook, M.D., and Leigh Cohn), it predicted that, as they became ever-more closely targeted by fashion brands and cosmetics companies, men would find themselves shouldering the pressures that were placed on women in the 1970s. 'In those days,' says the book, 'virtually *all* women wanted to be thinner. Eating disorders were increasing, in large part due to the culture's drive for thinness. Baby boomers, who had first been influenced by Twiggy and her lookalikes in the 60s, tried to find new ways to be willowy... Many turned to anorexia and bulimia, which was accompanied by low self-esteem, pervasive fear of weight gain, emotional emptiness, phobic avoidance of food and poor health. Diet books and plans were prevalent then, as they are now, and women's magazines... rarely went to press without a new diet on the cover.'

The authors worry that the objectification of male bodies is creating a similar landscape for men. Although male models have always existed, until recently they remained swathed in some kind of clothing. The book dates the beginning of the 'objectification' trend to 1992, when the rapper 'Marky' Mark Wahlberg appeared on a giant ad for Calvin Klein underwear in Times Square. He was clad only in briefs, heavily muscled and clutching his genitalia. 'Nothing was left to the imagination in this enormous billboard, including the genitals, which were prominently emphasized, but played peek-a-boo under the briefs being hawked. Few males,' claim the authors, 'could pass... Mark's almost naked body without being depressed by the comparative inadequacy of their own bodies.'

The authors argue that an emphasis on sculptural perfection – contrasted with the lack of exercise time available to 21st century executives – is creating an unspoken crisis among men. One of them, Thomas Holbrook, relates his own battle with anorexia. In a particularly terrifying image, we find him building a small pool in his basement and swimming on the spot, 'tethered to the wall' – literally a slave to his obsession. He over-exercises, under-eats and then binges, finally becoming a broken-down skeleton. Despite several hospital admissions, he is not diagnosed as anorexic. Was this, he asks, because at that time the disease was associated only with women? We now know that anorexia and bulimia are on the rise among men – but are the figures worse than we realise?

Unsurprisingly, the book recommends a balanced diet and regular, non-obsessive exercise as the keys to healthy living. Along the way, it points out that short-term dieting does not work. 'Most weight loss by dieting will be restored 12 months after stopping the diet, usually to a higher weight. Dieting is usually unpleasant, unnecessary, unhealthy and expensive... at a minimum, it creates havoc with a person's metabolism and wardrobe.'

Advertising is unswervingly blamed for provoking feelings of inadequacy among men. The authors identify four archetypes of images that target male consumers.

- *Bad boy/good body*: three-day stubble, carefully dishevelled hair, body-built torso and scowl.
- *Schizoid:* Scrawny and starved, distracted expression, dressed in tight-fitting designer clothing that appears ill-fitting but is in fact 'radically non-conformist'.
- *Preppy:* The pullover-on-the-shoulders, buttoned down, glossy Labrador-owning, country club brigade. You know who you are, Messrs Lauren and Hilfiger.
- *Rich, powerful and greedy:* Sober suit, black leather-soled shoes, shiny man bag, beautiful woman looking on admiringly.

These formulas may have been identified way back at the turn of the millennium, but they are still clearly recognizable.

The growing resistance to 'objectified' men in advertising seems to be filtering down to marketers, who have responded in a half-hearted fashion. 'Some menswear designers and fashion magazines are starting to choose male models who look more like "regular guys",' reported *The Wall Street Journal* in early 2007. The article quoted Sean Patterson, president of the Wilhelmina Models Agency, who confirmed, 'Designers are clearly more conscious that their consumer is a very, very broad spectrum of male.' ('Style and substance: designers target the regular guy', 2 February 2007.)

Of course, a model can never look like a 'regular guy', because ordinary men do not become models. As the article concurred, the models chosen were still 'mostly in their 20s' and were described as resembling Richard Gere, Tom Cruise or George Clooney. One commentator defined the look as, 'Chiselled without being too pretty.' But not too ordinary, either.

HOMME FATALE

A healthy interest in diet and exercise is no bad thing if men are to live longer. But there are signs that some men deceive themselves about the root causes of their weight problems. The YouGov report mentioned earlier said that rather than laying off the pizza and taking to the pool, men preferred to blame their expanding waistlines on their genetic make-up, the ageing process, or 'medical reasons beyond their control'. Unfortunately, this is one of the few occasions on which self-deception could turn out to be fatal. To use a phrase that is often picked up by the media, being a man is a health hazard.

Men die younger than women – and it's mostly due to their behaviour. In 2003, *Time* magazine reported on a study from the University of Michigan's Institute for Social Research. It said that in the United States, men outranked women in all of the 15 leading causes of death except one: Alzheimer's.

Of course, this phenomenon is linked to far more factors than diet, including tobacco and alcohol consumption, stress, dangerous working conditions – and even a taste for fast cars. ('Why men die young', 4 May 2003.) But the fact remains that cardiovascular disease (CVD) is one of the world's most efficient slayers of men. The World Health Organization says that more than 17 million people died of a cardiovascular illness such as a heart attack or a stroke in 2005 – that's almost 30 per cent of global deaths. A further 20 million people survive heart attacks every year. 'The rise in CVDs reflects a significant change in diet habits, physical activity levels, and tobacco consumption worldwide as a result of industrialization, urbanization, economic development and food market globalization.' ('Cardiovascular disease: prevention and control', www.who.int.) If men have been less concerned about their figures in the past, they've also been undisciplined about diet and exercise.

The danger is exacerbated by the fact that men stubbornly resist visiting the doctor – not only for check-ups, but also when they feel genuinely unwell. They consider stoicism one of the greatest virtues. As *The Observer* newspaper pointed out, the only medical check men can abide is one in which they are told: 'Your body has repelled an attack from an extremely rare virus that targets only the toughest people on Earth… You must now rest for a fortnight, eating and drinking whatever takes your fancy' ('The problem's doctors: be afraid, be very afraid', 27 November 2005).

The subject of the article was a survey carried out in the United Kingdom by the Men's Health Forum, which actively campaigns for a more sympathetic approach to men's healthcare issues. It revealed that men felt excluded from the medical system. 'They don't like explaining the reason they have come to a [female] receptionist; they find surgery hours inconvenient; they feel the whole system is geared towards women' – right down, they added, to the magazines in the waiting room. 'It makes you feel like you are sitting in a ladies' hairdressers,' one said. When asked to suggest improvements, men mooted smarter, more masculine décor and TVs screening classic movies. Doctors were rather dismissive of the comments, pointing out that nobody enjoyed visiting the doctor – and yet women still managed to drag themselves along.

At least one group heeded the men's plaintive cries, however. Health experts in Knowsley on Merseyside decided to hold medical check-ups at local pubs. 'Health advisers spend 40 minutes checking the health and lifestyle of each man, covering areas including blood pressure, cholesterol, smoking and drinking habits. Almost nine out of 10 participants make at least one healthy change in their lifestyle as a result, and most feel they received a good service, according to research by the University of Liverpool' ('A pint and a check-up please', *The Express*, 14 March 2006).

It may have attracted whimsical headlines, but this initiative is a step in the right direction. Experts have suggested that men are not being effectively communicated to when it comes to health issues. The University of Western Sydney's men's health expert, Professor John Macdonald, told the sixth national Men's Health Conference in Melbourne that 'behaving badly' was too often blamed for the relative ill health of men. 'This allows governments to avoid taking responsibility for men's poor health,' he said. He urged health authorities to embark on campaigns specifically targeted at men. 'We spend more time worrying about how to get Aussie men to do more housework than we do trying to understand why blokes continue to kill themselves in great numbers each year,' he said. ('What's killing men?', *Herald Sun*, 12 October 2005.)

His views supported those expressed in a 2001 World Health Organization paper called 'Men, Ageing and Health'. This confirms that a man's life expectancy remains, on average, five to eight years shorter than a woman's. It also lifts the veil on CVD and its impact on the sexes. The paper states that while CVD remains 'the most common single cause of death in old age in both sexes', older males 'suffer from higher incidences' of heart disease than females. 'Age-specific death rates for all cardiovascular diseases increase at least twofold between the age groups 65–74 years and 75–84 years in both sexes, with at least 50% higher rates for elderly men than for women.'

The paper dryly laments that the most important risk factors for cardiovascular disease – being male and elderly – cannot be modified. However, cigarette smoking, high blood pressure, elevated cholesterol and obesity can. The cornerstones for survival are a balanced diet (plenty of fruit and vegetables, whole grains, lean meat, fish and pulses, restricted sugar and salt intake), regular physical activity (at least 30 minutes every day) and quitting smoking.

Women successfully placed their health issues on the agenda in the 80s and 90s by intimating that healthcare communication was inherently biased and did not address their specific needs. Men have felt unable to make similar claims. As the paper puts it: 'The challenge involved in placing the concerns of men firmly on the health agenda is even greater, since it will entail orchestrating a fight in which there is no opponent, no oppressor. The battle will be against complacency, against established attitudes, towards a culture in which men would recognize the importance of looking after themselves, a culture of self-care, as opposed to the current common belief of men who regard themselves as "indestructible machines".'

This void has largely been filled by the fitness industry rather than health authorities. Men are joining expensive gyms and succumbing to obscure diets. A couple of years ago, *The Times* reported on people who believed that extreme calorie restriction – known as CR – could prolong their lives. 'Some practitioners confidently expect to live to 130,' the article said. It introduced us to Dave, 48, who 'with superhuman discipline' stuck to 'an intake of 1,600 calories a day, well below the 2,550 that the British Nutrition Foundation recommends for men'. Members of the Calorie Restriction Society in California (www.calorierestriction. org), the newspaper found, were 'overwhelmingly male'. The article also told us that one of the founders of the society, Roy Walford, author of *The 120-Year Diet*, died at the age of 79, of motor neurone disease ('Eat less – and live to 130', 3 October 2005).

The media regularly confront us with news of foods that may or may not increase our lifespan. Red wine is good for us. Garlic is good for us. Green tea is good for us. Tomatoes are good for us. Dark chocolate is good for us. At the time of writing, Brazil nuts were all the rage: they contain selenium, which is said to enhance sperm production. Even male-pattern baldness, that genetic curse, has been linked to diet. 'Some researchers suspect high-fat diets can contribute to hair loss – especially diets with low-hydrogenated fats, found in processed-meat convenience products such as pies, pastries and sausage rolls, and some margarines and spreadable fats. A diet high in essential fatty acids – found in fish, nuts and seeds – may have the reverse effect.' ('Create your own man-sized diet', *Business Day*, South Africa, 4 April 2007.)

Products that directly target men's stomachs – or rather, an urge to reduce them – are appearing with increasing regularity. In the summer of 2006, Coca-Cola launched what the press was quick to dub 'bloke Coke': Coca-Cola Zero. It abandoned the brand's traditional red and white packaging in favour of a sleek black livery. Coke's biggest new product launch for 22 years, it was created as a male alternative to Diet Coke, which men had always regarded as a bit girlie. As we know, men dislike the word 'diet', so Coke used the term 'zero calories'. A spokesman said: 'The [packaging] complements boys' toys like BlackBerries, mobile phones and PSPs and we think will appeal to this audience... while Diet Coke continues to satisfy a wide audience, particularly women, who love the taste.' ('Bloke Coke: Diet drink gets macho name and black can to appeal to young males', *Daily Record*, 13 May 2006.)

The launch utilized an array of marketing techniques, including an online campaign in the United States that played on the drink's similarity in flavour to that of regular Coke (as opposed to, crucially, Diet Coke). Customers who couldn't tell the difference were encouraged to sue the company for 'taste infringement'. In the United Kingdom, a TV ad used the slogan, 'Why can't all the good things in life come without the downsides?' This was a somewhat less original approach, as advertising anoraks who remember the 1990s Müller Light yoghurt commercials with comedians Vic Reeves and Bob Mortimer will tell you ('Pleasure without the pain').

Essentially, though, the launch of Coca-Cola Zero was a taste of things to come: a diet product aimed very specifically at men.

BRANDING TOOLKIT

- Men don't 'diet'.

- But they are concerned about body image.

- Hence a rising number of male-targeted 'healthy' food products.

- There is increasing resistance to the 'objectification' of the male body.

- Also a need for authoritative, coherent information about healthy eating.

- As they abandon fast food, men are becoming comfortable with cooking.

- They admire 'role model' chefs.

- There is a growing male market for cook-books and kitchen equipment.

4

Home

Scene Four: The Living Room

On the way out, he scoops his car keys from the white glazed earthenware bowl on the low bookcase that lines one side of the living room. On the same surface there are several framed photographs and a slender glass vase that has rarely held flowers. An old Gitanes ashtray that he no longer uses is a souvenir of a visit to a Paris flea-market. As you might expect, the décor of his home is neutral and uncluttered. Fresh white walls, cream linen curtains, black and white prints by French and American photographers. There's also a vintage poster of the Steve McQueen film *Le Mans*, which he bought at the Movie Poster Art Gallery in the West End.

The furniture comes from two major sources: Habitat and Ikea. For more expensive purchases he likes The Conran Shop, Heal's and BoConcept. Unobtrusively tasteful pieces are augmented by items he collected on his travels: rugs from Marrakech and Istanbul; a brass Buddha from Hong Kong, a shisha pipe from Egypt; two watercolour street scenes he picked up in Prague after spotting them in an antique shop window. A toy New York taxicab is parked on one of the bookshelves. The books range from Dan Brown thrillers to the latest Man Booker Prize winner, alongside glossy art and photography tomes and business paperbacks. A ragged pile of newspapers and magazines sprawls on the low coffee table. There are other signs of individuality: cushions in solid colours brighten the tan leather club chair from Habitat and the 'Loft' four-seat sofa from Conran, upholstered in charcoal felted wool. There's also the giant orange beanbag he sometimes uses for watching a movie or the match in front of his Sony Bravia.

He'd love to do more with the place, but during the week he's barely there. And at the weekend, he's usually too tired to shop for home furnishings.

SINGLE LIFE

If men are more at home in the kitchen these days, they're also developing more of an eye for their homes. This is undoubtedly linked to the rise in the number of men who live alone. In Britain and the United States, the solo lifestyle is becoming increasingly common. In the US, the proportion of single households rose from 17 per cent in 1970 to 26 per cent in 2005 (US Census Bureau press release, 25 May 2006). And in the United Kingdom, the number of households with just one person has increased by 31 per cent over roughly the same period, according to a 2005 study by the Economic and Social Research Council (www.esrc.ac.uk).

Another British organization, the Institute for Public Policy Research (IPPR) believes that by 2021, more than 35 per cent of all households will consist of one person. And this trend is being driven by men: 15 per cent of men aged between 25 and 44 live alone, as opposed to 8 per cent of women. But just as it would be wrong to assume that the women are all lonely, Chardonnay-swigging 'singletons' like the fictional Bridget Jones, it would be foolish to assume that the men resemble her philandering occasional lover, Daniel Cleaver.

'Women enter into [single living] with more gusto, they see it as a mark of independence and a means of expanding their social network,' says Melissa Lewis, author of the IPPR Unilever Family Report 2005. 'A lot more men find it lonely. It is the daily contact they miss most, particularly not having someone to talk to at the end of a bad day at work.' ('Home alone', *BBC News Magazine*, 27 October 2005.)

While some solo men have girlfriends and enjoy 'the best of both worlds', Lewis stressed that 'the stereotype of the white, middle-class person living in a loft apartment is not the reality'. Living alone is expensive, and only a small percentage of people are rich enough to 'cushion themselves from the asset shocks... and are more likely to feel that the expense is worth it'.

There are also fears that more solo living could have a negative impact on the environment. Demand for housing will grow and the larger number of single households will lead to increased energy consumption. The IPPR suggests that the trend towards single households needs to be more seriously addressed by governments and incorporated into environmental and social planning. 'The impact of solo living is still very much unknown,' Lewis told the BBC. 'The government and industry need to get thinking.'

The makers of domestic appliances, of course, see solo living as a marketing opportunity. In September 2007, Electrolux took the unusual step of releasing a book called *Men in Aprons*, which it sold on its website. Written by a 30-year-old female journalist, the frothy novel related the travails of a housework-hating man who was forced to fend for himself when his girlfriend moved out of their apartment – taking all the appliances with her. Each chapter ended with handy household tips courtesy of Electrolux. The book format was designed to get around the fact that young men are becoming harder to reach with TV advertising. The campaign had several elements working against it. The first, and most obvious, is that men don't like to think of themselves as incompetents in aprons. The second is that books are not the best way of reaching men (see Chapter 7). Even the stereotype of the housework-shy male seemed tired.

On the contrary, a certain type of man regards his apartment as a powerful self-branding tool. Just as his clothes are selected to express his personality, and the way he wishes to be regarded by others, his home is a shell encapsulating his identity. The alluring concept of 'the bachelor pad' has existed for many years. In the stories of E.W. Hornung, written in the late Victorian/early Edwardian period, the gentleman thief Raffles keeps 'rooms' in The Albany, a mansion off Piccadilly converted into what is essentially a grand block of apartments. The concept of bachelordom as a viable lifestyle option was more actively hawked by Hugh Hefner, founder of *Playboy* magazine, in the 1950s. But the martini-swigging, Manhattan-dwelling existence of the playboy was a fantasy, and the reality of New York bachelor life was considerably grimmer. The masterly black comedy *The Apartment* (1960) uses this contrast to great effect. While the neighbours of C.C. 'Buddy' Baxter (Jack Lemmon) imagine that he's a cool swinger, seducing a different chick every night, in fact he's augmenting his meagre income by letting out his place to married executives who need somewhere to 'entertain' their mistresses. When we catch him home alone, Baxter knocks about the grey little apartment, so ill-adapted to single living that he drains spaghetti through a tennis racket.

But the film also reflects the fact that, in those days, the bachelor was a somewhat marginal figure. Today, he's moved into the mainstream – whether young and starting out or divorced and starting again. The *Financial Times* carried a profile of two wealthy young bachelors – both investment bankers – who'd teamed up to buy a mews house, so they could turn it into a dream home and thus attract girlfriends.

'They had it gutted, re-built and fitted with an extra floor at top and bottom; installed a cinema, a hot tub and two garages… This wasn't some shabby old bloke-house, full of mouldering socks and cigarette-singed carpets; it was an architectural magazine centre-spread... Most of their furniture came from Italy, with the exception of a £2,500 David Linley leather chair inspired by classic Aston Martin cars. A mirrored central stairwell was an inspired touch, adding both light and a sense of space.' ('Privilege of a city slicker: bachelor pads have come a long way since the 19th century', 13 February 2007.)

And this is not just a London – or New York – thing. The *FT*'s report confirmed that bachelor pads were hot property from Cardiff to Hong Kong.

Even when he's moved in with his girlfriend – or wife – the branded male no longer surrenders the home-making process to his partner. His father may have turned a blind eye to the chintz and the cerise, but not him. Nesting has become a shared experience. As long ago as 1998, *The New York Times* identified 'The Wallpaper Generation'. Referring to the upmarket design magazine that had become a publishing phenomenon, the appellation concerned affluent urban couples who'd traded up in their taste in home furnishings. They were the kind of bourgeois bohemians who 'one day... put their funky votive candles and wrought-iron bed into storage and painted their natural-wood floors a lacquered black. They filled their Chelsea apartment with such modernica as a fibreglass 50s Tulip chair by Eero Saarinen, a shag rug, an amoeba-shaped coffee table and two space age chrome lamps they found on the Internet'. ('Generation Wallpaper', 6 September 1998.)

Firmly mid-century modern, the style was more accessible than it looked, thanks to a revolution that had begun in Europe.

HABITAT'S DAD

Any British person who has lived alone is likely to have found themselves wandering around a branch of Habitat – or, even more likely, Ikea – at least once, if not many times. Both brands are fascinating, and their recent histories are intertwined.

Habitat was created in 1964 by Terence Conran (now *Sir* Terence), the lifestyle guru and entrepreneur who has had an immeasurable impact on the tastes of the British middle classes. Conran's philosophy that 'Useful can be beautiful and beautiful can be affordable' recalls the 'democratic design' ideology of Ikea.

Born in 1931, Conran showed a natural aptitude for crafts at school. After studying at London's Central School of Art, he began making his own furniture in a cramped East End workshop, delivering items personally via the London Underground. Conran was also interested in food, and once did a stint as a *plongeur* – a dish-washer – at a Paris restaurant. In 1953, Conran and a group of friends opened The Soup Kitchen, a bohemian-chic restaurant rigged out with tiled floors, cane chairs and a Gaggia coffee machine. It sold mugs of soup with French bread and cheeses, cleverly repackaging European style for the Brits in a manner that has become a Conran signature. Eventually there were four branches – and Conran opened a more ambitious restaurant called The Orrery in King's Road.

All this time, he continued making furniture – but he was frustrated by the lack of appropriate retail spaces and the unimaginative way in which stores marketed his wares. It occurred to him that there was a niche for a different kind of home store that catered to the creative, freewheeling young consumers of the sixties. In an interview with *The Guardian*, Conran recalled: 'I was sitting with Pagan Taylor, the wife of an architect I knew, in her flat in Cadogan Square, and I said: "Pagan, get out Roget's Thesaurus, look up home and read out what it says". So she read it out and when it came to habitat, I said "stop, that's it. *Habitat*."' ('Old Habitats die hard', 22 December 2001.)

The first branch of Habitat opened in 1964 at 77 Fulham Road, London. In a stylish open-plan space, it sold Conran's furniture as well as pieces from France, Italy and Scandinavia. Consumers could furnish their homes with simple pine tables, beds and bookcases, affordable cutlery, and quirkier design items like beanbags or cool Bauhaus chairs. In short, the Habitat universe was a synthesis of the European style that Conran admired, and the unfussy yet bohemian look that his target consumers desired. This new market of university graduates and young entrepreneurs had discovered the Riviera, Tuscany and Marrakech – or at least fantasized about such places. They did not want their homes to resemble those of their parents – gloomy, heavy-curtained dens that had barely evolved since the 1940s – and Conran provided the first accessible alternative. Soon the store was attracting fashionable customers like Julie Christie, Michael Caine, Peter Sellers, Twiggy and Justin de Villeneuve, Sandy Shaw and Jeff Banks.

'For the first time, customers were encouraged to browse, to pick the goods off the shelves, and the range meant that even if you could not afford a Chesterfield sofa, you could always leave with a wooden spoon or lampshade. Regardless of budget, anyone could be part of the Habitat world.' ('Conran returns to his natural Habitat', *The Scotsman*, 3 December 2002.)

The store's rise coincided with the appearance of the newspaper colour supplement, which – along with the catalogue – proved one of its most valuable marketing tools. Now it could stage-manage the dream almost as effectively as it did in its own retail spaces. By the end of the 1960s, there were five branches of Habitat in London. Over the next decade, the store's style filtered into the mainstream. The author Jonathan Meades told *The Guardian*: '[Conran's] real achievement is to have popularized modernism. What you've got today is a synthetic modernism looking back at Le Corbusier and Goldfinger and even the brutalists. But it has become acceptable and user-friendly. He has taken modernism into the mainstream. He may have diluted it, but he, more than anyone, has changed British taste over the past 40 years. Think what houses looked like in the 50s.'

In 1981, Habitat merged with Mothercare, a retailer catering to the parents of young children. A further acquisition, of British Home Stores, led to the creation of a holding company called Storehouse. But this ultimately lost its creative edge, becoming corporate and soulless, and Conran gradually relinquished control. He stepped down as chairman in 1990 and the merged group broke up. Habitat was sold to Ingka Holding, the company that owns Ikea. By then, Conran had plenty of other outlets for his creativity, including several branches of The Conran Shop – a more luxurious take on Habitat – a number of upmarket restaurants, a design and architecture business and a publishing concern. In the *Guardian* article mentioned earlier, he said of Ikea: 'Bringing good design to the mass market is what I tried to do at Habitat but, as I can see now, I barely scratched the surface. I softened the ground for Ikea, but they made it happen.'

IKEA BOYS

The position of Ikea as the shrine of the single man was firmly established by the film *Fight Club* (1999). Among other things, the movie is about a man's quest to reactivate his suppressed masculinity. Along the way, it offers a harsh, if facile, critique of consumerism. In an early scene, as the camera pans across the hero's apartment, price-tags pop out of each newly-acquired piece of furniture as though we're looking at an Ikea catalogue. In another shot, the hero sits on the toilet with an Ikea catalogue in one hand and a mobile phone in the other, explaining in a voice-off: 'Like so many others, I had become a slave to the Ikea nesting instinct. If I saw something clever, like a little coffee table in the shape of a yin-yang, I had to have it... I'd flip through catalogues and wonder: which dining set defines me as a person?' The character is referred to as 'Ikea Boy', a phrase that was adopted by the media. The film (and the book that inspired it) seemed to be saying that tastefully decorated apartments were among the emasculating accoutrements of the 21st century.

For any guy who's ever found himself in an empty apartment that requires a bed, a sofa and a wardrobe – fast – Ikea is quite another thing. If we agree that living alone is expensive, then Ikea is the affordable solution that Habitat no longer represents.

Ikea was founded in 1943 in the southern Swedish province of Småland by the 17-year-old Ingvar Kamprad. The capital came from his father, a gift acknowledging his academic success. The name Ikea is contracted from Kamprad's own initials, plus those of Elmtaryd and Agunnaryd, the farm and village where he grew up. Initially it was a mail-order service. Kamprad specialized in identifying the needs of local citizens and fulfilling them with accessibly priced products: picture frames, pens, key-rings, nylons and so on. He'd save money and increase profit margins by having them delivered on the back of the milk truck. Furniture, produced by local manufacturers in the forests close to Kamprad's home, was introduced in 1947. It proved such a success that he was soon able to pull out of other product sectors and make it the focus of the company.

In 1955, two events occurred that were to make Kamprad's fortune. Angered by the way that Ikea was undercutting their prices, Swedish furniture dealers threatened to boycott suppliers who did business with the company. This ultimately severed Ikea's ties with local manufacturers and forced it to begin designing furniture in-house, as well as sourcing material from Eastern Europe. But the second event – although it seemed trivial at the time – proved even more significant. In order to save space when delivering a table, an employee removed its legs and tucked them underneath. Hey presto! Flat-packed furniture had been invented. This reduced the bulk – and therefore the cost – of shipping. It also took the responsibility for assembling items out of the hands of the furniture supplier, placing it firmly into those of the often baffled consumer. In effect, by tacitly agreeing to do part of the work themselves, customers were keeping the prices down. It was the key that unlocked a global market for the company, now based in Älmhult, not far from where Kamprad grew up.

Like H&M – the Swedish firm that has democratized fashion – Ikea's expansion has been driven by rock-bottom prices, frill-free products and efficient distribution. In 1973, Kamprad wrote a document called 'The Testament of a Furniture Dealer', in which he spoke of the company's 'duty to expand'. Now he'd figured out how to transport his products cheaply, everyone should have the right to enjoy them. The philosophy of democratic design was not new – indeed, it was being espoused by everyone from Terence Conran to the Italian furniture designer Joe Colombo – but this was the first time it had become truly achievable.

'The high priests of design preached a democratic ethos; in reality, they never got much further than the upper-middle classes,' observes *The Guardian*. ('The miracle of Älmhult', 17 June 2004.) The article points out that by the time Ikea opened its first British store, in 1987, 'Habitat had grown lazy and the market was wide open'. Thatcher's Britons were setting up home and they wanted interiors that equalled their yuppie aspirations. Heavy, varnished antiques in dark wood were unlikely to appeal to them: they wanted furniture that was streamlined, dynamic and conspicuously 'new'.

Although Kamprad has now stepped back from day-to-day control of the company, he remains heavily influential. Its parent, Ingka Holding, belongs to the Stichting Ingka Foundation, a Dutch-registered charitable organization whose mission is to encourage innovation in the field of architectural and interior design. It also maintains a large reserve to cater for Ikea's future capital expenditure. At the time of writing, there are 258 Ikea stores in 35 countries and territories. Annual sales total 17.3 billion euros. More amusing is the oft-quoted 'fact' that 10 per cent of Europeans have been conceived on an Ikea bed. Way to go, Ikea Boy!

Much has been made of our love–hate relationship with Ikea, as we lug items home to spend hours searching fruitlessly for missing screws and cursing impenetrable instructions. But the brand has wormed its way into our affections with a series of cunning, humorous advertising campaigns, many of which satirize its cult-like image. A 1997 campaign urging Britons to 'chuck out the chintz' featured homeowners hysterically ripping apart their cluttered, stifling interiors to make way for streamlined Ikea furniture. A later series featured three vaguely sinister Scandinavians, who turned up in people's homes to warn them about the dangers of avoiding Ikea and being condemned to a life of tastelessness ('Come and see us, before we come and see you'). Even when you can painfully recall standing in your living room surrounded by islands of mismatched wood, it's difficult to hate a company that knows how to laugh at itself.

Despite its popularity with young men, Ikea says it does not make products specifically for them. 'In fact our ranges are developed to provide solutions to different living situations,' says the brand's UK home furnishings specialist, Emma Carson. 'So that might be single living, starting out as a couple, or an established family.' However, she accepts that as Ikea products are 'practical and strongly influenced by the urban environment' they are bound to appeal to men. 'In addition, small-space living is a long-term priority for Ikea,' she adds.

In terms of how they think about interiors, Carson says men are more attuned to design than they were a decade ago. 'A whole generation has been brought up with interior decorating shows like *Changing Rooms* and *Location, Location, Location*,' she points out. 'They're much more sophisticated, and the days of the loutish bachelor pad are over. Investing in a comfortable home tends to be fairly high on their agenda.'

Not that men don't have specific needs. Technology looms large in their lives and Carson says they don't always mentally separate it from the rest of their surroundings. 'They'll think about a sofa in terms of how it will work with the position of the hi-fi and the television. Some of them want to create a sort of "media station" effect.' Indeed, 'Live technologically' is one of the exhortations on the Ikea website.

Younger men living away from home for the first time appreciate unobtrusive furniture that seamlessly blends in with items donated by their parents. 'Flexibility and portability is important, because they're often living in rented accommodation and they want things they can take with them. But the style aspect is equally important because they're sociable and this is their first experience of entertaining in their own homes.'

Perhaps an even more valuable marketing device than the advertising mentioned above is the Ikea catalogue. A total of 175 million copies are printed each year – more than the Bible, at an estimated 100,000 million – in 55 editions and 26 different languages. It is shot in a studio in Älmhult, with each set constructed to ensure that the furniture takes on a Hollywood splendour. The Ikea website – for online ordering – takes its cue from the catalogue in presenting seductive yet affordable rooms. Many buyers still brave the weekend traffic to visit Ikea's town perimeter stores, however.

'Each store is different,' says Carson. 'We research the typical profile of the customer in the area where the store is based, and design our room settings accordingly. People like to come and see how an item of furniture would look in real life.'

Among the products that particularly appeal to male customers are those in the Ikea Stockholm collection – pale and brutally simple – and the younger Ikea P.S. range – modular and colourful, including metallic locker-style cabinets in fire-engine red, silver or white. Another winner is the Karlstad swivel armchair in grey or orange: a moulded polyurethane model that screams Scandinavian hip. 'It's a very competitively-priced piece that effectively illustrates the idea of democratic design,' Carson adds.

In the past, an item of furniture had a metaphorical as well as a physical weight – there was a good chance a chest of drawers would be passed on to the next generation. Thanks to Ikea and its imitators, homes have become playgrounds for self-expression.

Furniture is as disposable as fashion. Today, a wardrobe is as ephemeral as the clothes it contains. And for the young male shopper still uncertain of his taste, that's just fine.

BRANDING TOOLKIT

- Single living is on the rise.

- Bachelors express their identities through their homes.

- Naturally, they use their apartments to impress potential mates.

- Furniture is expected to blend with technology.

- Household objects have become as disposable as fashion.

- Advice and inspiration are greatly appreciated.

- Men in relationships want an equal say in home furnishings.

- The catalogue and website are key communications vectors.

5

Wheels

Scene Five: The Street

The company BMW 335i Coupe is sleeping in the 'residents only' parking slot across the road from his Clapham flat. Although he's not a car fanatic, he's aware that BMW designer Chris Bangle is a controversial figure, often taking the German giant's styling in unexpected directions. But this BMW isn't remarkably different to the others he's driven in his life: unpretentious good looks, an unfussy yet comfortable interior that recalls a business class airline cabin, an engine that ambles smoothly around town when required – and delivers a turbo-powered punch on the *autobahn*. Somehow he can't imagine himself driving a sporty soft-top. Apart from the fact that he can still hear his father referring to them as 'hairdressers' cars', he associates them with rich kids posing on King's Road, or overweight bastards experiencing midlife crises. Having said that, he enjoys driving his girlfriend's Mini Cooper, and he has noted the restyled Fiat 500's saucy charm.

He clips himself into the BMW and fires her up. Driving to work is a ridiculous indulgence – especially since he has to catch a train to Paris later that day. But he can no longer bring himself to use London's broken-down underground system, and the congestion charge has made the journey to his Soho office marginally less nightmarish. The BMW handles so well that even these short hops are pleasurable. Plus he can catch up with the news and listen to a bit of music.

As he glides past the Common (still some joggers out; where do they work?) he clicks on the radio. The soothing tones of the *Today* programme on BBC Radio 4 fill the car. He knows without looking at his watch that he's got about three minutes before the sports update. Afterwards, he listens to a bit of news and discussion. 'War and rumours of war,' he mutters and switches to the pop chewing gum of Capital FM, 'London's hit music station' for as long as he can remember. He likes to keep in touch with the stuff in the charts: it gives him the impression that he understands young people.

By the time the BMW has homed in on Soho, the station's breath-less pace and raucous ads have begun to wear him down. He cuts the music when he reaches the car park on Poland Street, where he'll leave the BMW overnight at a cost of £35 – which thankfully will come out of his expenses.

UPWARDLY AUTOMOBILE

Will men ever stop loving cars? Despite traffic congestion, guilt over global warming and the strangulation of machismo, it seems unlikely. Our attraction to these glossy machines is atavistic. We push toy cars around on the carpet when we're kids. We enjoy watching them racing, jousting and crashing in movies. When we're teenagers, we can't wait to roar off in our first cars as soon as we've passed our tests. Very often, we then tune and modify them until they are an expression of the power and status we feel we need.

'Modding' or 'tuning' cars is popular on both sides of the Atlantic. An article in *Newsweek* claimed that US college students repre-sented a US$15 million market, purchasing one in 10 new cars. And, it added, they were spending a further US$4.2 billion a year customizing them. Inspired by movies like *The Fast and the Furious* and the MTV show *Pimp My Ride*, 'they're outfitting their rides with ground-shaking sound systems, nitrous-injected engines and 20-inch rims... ' Although the article doesn't say so, the reader is left with the impression that the trend is almost exclusively male. Take Erick, who spent US$4000 customizing his black Toyota Scion tC by 'lowering it, beefing up the suspension and adding red "underglow" interior lights and high-intensity headlights'. Erick says proudly: 'A lot of cars can out-power me, but I can outmanoeuvre them.' Elsewhere, the article mentions a Texas A&M University student whose 'silver 75 Firebird with black racing stripes' is 'such a head-turner, several female students have even... offered him some back-seat action in return for a ride' ('Hot wheels', August 21–28, 2006). When you talk about men and cars, it isn't long before sex enters the equation.

Do more men own cars than women? That's certainly the case in the UK, according to research by TGI, analysed by Mintel. 'TGI data reveals a residual gender gap in car ownership, with around 79% of men versus 67% of women owning a car.' (Car Market Aspirations, UK, 2006.) But the gender gap on the roads is closing, and Mintel feels that 'the residual male bias in car ownership points to the generation gap in car ownership whereby it would not have been the norm for women currently aged 65+ to learn to drive, but to have relied on their male partner as the family driver'.

What is incontestable is that men approach cars and driving in an entirely different manner to women. As the trend tracking organization Style-Vision puts it, 'Men love machines because they reflect and flatter [two aspects of] the masculine mystique: performance and independence.' (Megatrend No. 10: Men.) Later, the report adds: 'The classic ideal of masculinity relies on four stereotypes that men feel obliged to comply with: the requirement to neutralize the feminine side of their emotions, the demand to be successful, admired and powerful, the necessity to be independent, and finally the commitment to be strong and fearless. Most men are now conscious that heavy doses of these masculine stereotypes can be toxic for them. But they love cars. That's all.'

The general consensus is that, when asked to describe their ideal car, women would cite practicality, affordability and design flair, while men would go for luxury and power. The reality is somewhat more complex. When the publisher Condé Nast surveyed 2,500 British motorists on their attitudes to car buying in 2006, it found that both sexes rated 'reliability' as the most important characteristic of an automobile, followed by safety, security, comfort and price. Style and design came sixth out of ten possible options. More women than men said that they were 'emotionally attached' to their vehicles, but this could be just another example of the male need to appear implacable. In contrast, far fewer men (49 per cent versus 63 per cent) thought that speed cameras had a beneficial effect on road safety. This sits logically with the fact that 84 per cent of the men surveyed wanted the speed limit increased on motorways. Hardly any women did. Men associate speed not only with excitement, but with mastery of the vehicle – another way to demonstrate their control over the machine.

Amusingly, many male respondents to the Condé Nast survey did not feel that women were neglected by car marketers, with 75 per cent of women agreeing that 'car adverts don't recognize the role of women in the process of car buying', as opposed to 59 per cent of men. But the fact is that women are often ignored by car advertisers – and quite deliberately so.

Uwe Ellinghaus, marketing director of BMW UK, says: 'It is my strong conviction that women are no more of a target group than men are. In fact, most automobile brands target a homogeneous group that shares certain characteristics. When it comes to positioning a brand, gender matters less and less. The same could be said for age. What you will notice, though, is that automobile brands are keen to avoid giving cars a feminine image. Once a car is viewed as "a chick's car", no man will touch it, and then you have a marketing problem on your hands. You'll notice, therefore, that when we portray typical drivers, they are mostly male. This does not jar with women drivers, who are often businesswomen whose demands and aspirations are those more typically associated with male consumers.'

This view is backed by David Kiley's excellent (2004) book *Driven: Inside BMW, The Most Admired Car Company in the World*. Kiley quotes Hennie Chung, BMW North America's executive in charge of developing the BMW Z4. Its predecessor, the Z3, although mostly bought by males, had been saddled with a somewhat feminine image. 'Toward the end of the Z3's cycle, we had the stigma of being a "girlie car",' she admits. Heung explains that men 'will not buy what they view as a "pink" car, but women will always buy a car with a masculine image'.

Asked to define the image of BMW, Ellinghaus speaks of 'sporty-ness, dynamism, innovative design and refined interiors', all of which are encapsulated by the brand's two famous slogans: 'Sheer Driving Pleasure', used in Europe, and 'The Ultimate Driving Machine', coined by a US advertising agency in the 1970s. 'Our cars are designed in such a way that they look like they're being driven even when they're standing still,' says Ellinghaus. 'There could be a strong relationship between this dynamism and the sense of aggressiveness that is associated with young males, but in fact our market is not at all the young, reckless driver.'

In his book, David Kiley describes a typical BMW owner in the United States. 'In mid-2001, two-thirds of BMW customers were male; the average BMW customer was 46 years old; median income was US$150,000; the majority were well-educated, married and had no children.'

Kiley interviews a 43-year-old BMW owner, whose home is stocked with high-end equipment like a Bose stereo system and a Viking stove. The consumer responds: 'Brand-conscious? Yes. Snob? Maybe some people think so. But I have high-end appliances because I respect the products I buy, that I surround myself with. I cook a lot. I entertain pretty frequently. I love my BMW 530i. I love driving it. When I drive a car every day, as I do, I want to feel that it is more than just a conveyance.'

BRANDING THE 'BIMMER'

BMW has thrived the way all great brands do: by making a concrete, easily understandable claim, and then busting a gut to live up to it. While Chris Bangle's designs have not always delighted the motoring press, reviews concerning the performance of BMW's automobiles are overwhelmingly positive. Today the association of BMW with great handling is so ingrained that it's easy to forget that the brand didn't really come into its own until the 1970s.

In 1896 an aircraft company based just outside Munich opened a small automobile factory in Eisenach. It produced an odd but, in its day, highly regarded electric vehicle called the Wartburg. This was followed by several models of a car called the Dixi, which eventually lent its name to the company. Dixi was intermittently successful until 1927, when it struck a deal with the British car firm Austin to produce the highly successful Austin Seven as a Dixi under licence. At around the same time, Dixi owner Jakob Shapiro sold the company to motorcycle and aero-engine builder Bayerische Motoren Werke. BMW's roots in aeronautics can still be detected in its logo, which represents a propeller against a blue Bavarian sky. The Dixi was renamed the BMW 3/15 and became a bestseller. As David Kiley writes, 'So BMW's first motorcar experience was not hatched in the workshops of its own clever engineers, but in the factories and design studios of Great Britain.'

As we'll discover, it was not the last time the German company would achieve success with a car that had its roots in the UK. Meanwhile, though, BMW had to survive another world war and the distinctly depressed 1950s, when the company veered between making overblown luxury saloons and the quirky Isetta micro-car – a bubble-shaped three-wheeler powered by a motorcycle engine. Fortunately, the company was then acquired by the Quandt family of German industrialists, who pressured it into producing a 'decent, reliable, midrange car'. Launched at the 1961 Frankfurt Motor Show, the resulting BMW – the 1500 – set the company on the road to brand glory. With its aggressive, shark-like appearance, 'near-perfect' balance and impressive handling, the 1500 formed a template for BMWs to come. 'BMW's future formula was clear,' writes David Kiley. 'Four doors, room for five, a sporty engine, fine handling, neat styling, and high-speed *autobahn* capability.'

Kiley praises BMW for its consistency as a brand since that time. Other marques have also achieved longevity by ploughing a consistent furrow. Think of the plucky reliability of Volkswagen ('If only everything in life was as reliable as a Volkswagen') and the safety-first image of Volvo: a classic print ad from 1991 simply shows a great white shark circling a diver in a cage, above the caption, 'Cages save lives: Volvo'. For Volvo drivers, aesthetics are secondary – what they seek is protection for themselves and their families.

In early 1970s America, BMW was still a cult brand, appreciated by the cognoscenti but little known outside a fairly niche group of fans. Its advertising messages, diffused by a variety of importers, were confused. And so, in 1974, BMW centralized its sales and marketing and began looking for an advertising agency that could give it a unified brand identity. It eventually hired an upcoming young shop called Ammirati & Puris.

Ralph Ammirati and Martin Puris had sprung indirectly out of the 'creative revolution' of the late fifties and early sixties, which took influence away from the monolithic Madison Avenue agencies and placed it in the hands of a younger, hipper, more irreverent crowd. An agency called Doyle Dane Bernbach had done wonders for the Volkswagen brand with a series of witty print ads that broke all the rules, becoming entertainment in their own right. (The most famous, headlined 'Think Small', showed a tiny Beetle on an almost blank page.) Could Ammirati & Puris do the same thing for BMW?

Martin Puris told David Kiley: 'The cars handled like no other. That was for sure… The chassis on a BMW was a beautiful thing compared with other makes of the day. It was like driving on rails compared with Fiat and Volvos, or Mercedes, for that matter. So we had the strategy of always emphasizing handling and driving pleasure.'

The line the agency came up with was, of course, 'The Ultimate Driving Machine'. This bold statement would enable BMW to ride the new wave of print advertising, which was growing increasingly visual as the 'long copy' of the previous decades slowly withered. Puris said: 'I knew, among other things, that it would be great on billboards and bus shelters to just run a picture of the car with that one line of copy if we wanted to, without any other copy.'

More than just a slogan, over the next decade 'The Ultimate Driving Machine' became a mission statement that informed everything the company did. Its European adaptation, 'Sheer Driving Pleasure', was merely another expression of the same idea. Crucially, for our purposes, it spoke directly to everything men love about driving: control, power, and the surging thrill they feel in the pit of their stomachs as they apply pressure to the accelerator.

WEB FOR HIRE

BMW's most famous advertising campaign can trace its lineage back to the 1980s, and the era of the yuppie. With its air of discreet luxury, the BMW was the perfect accessory for the young, upwardly mobile consumer who wanted to express his new-found wealth without resorting to the flashy gimmickry of the conventional *nouveaux riches*. But while the BMW became the ultimate yuppie vehicle, this new target group initially presented a marketing challenge to BMW. Highly active individuals with busy social lives, yuppies didn't hang around in one place long enough to catch many TV ads – and although they taped shows that they liked, they fast-forwarded through the ads while catching up on their viewing. In this respect, yuppies were the forerunners of today's technology-savvy consumers, who use personal video recorders to skip ad breaks.

During the eighties, when the internet was still a shadowy grid of interconnected computers known only to academics, the solution for BMW was print advertising – in the business pages and in the glossy men's magazines that the yuppie male was now consuming. But by the late 1990s, active and highly mobile consumers could be targeted with an entirely new medium.

The first truly successful example of branded entertainment on the web almost ended up being shown at the cinema. In 2000, BMW had a new agency, Fallon, and a new goal: to go beyond conventional TV and print advertising. During meetings, two separate strategies emerged. One was to make a series of short films to be shown in movie theatres, while the other was to advertise on the internet. At a certain point, these two ideas fused into the inspired concept of creating a series of spectacular action movies for the web. Research had shown that consumers under the age of 50 were spending more time online than watching TV – and as many as 85 per cent of potential BMW consumers used the internet to research their purchases. In addition, web advertising would have a niche, technologically-aware slant that was likely to appeal to the BMW target group.

Fallon and BMW decided to go all-out and attach top Hollywood directors to the project. It was the only way, they reasoned, to ensure that the films would be taken seriously while adhering to the brand's quality image. The task proved easier than they expected: directors such as David Fincher (*Fight Club*), John

Frankenheimer (*Ronin*), Ang Lee (*Crouching Tiger, Hidden Dragon*), Guy Richie (*Snatch*) and Wong Kar-Wai (*In the Mood for Love*) were enthusiastic about having a crack at a new medium. Clive Owen would play the hero of the films, the mysterious 'driver', who is hired to transport various dodgy individuals to their destinations and invariably needs his trusty BMW to steer him out of trouble. Hence the name of the series: *The Hire*. Unusually, the car company gave the directors carte blanche in terms of how they would treat – or rather, mistreat – its automobiles during the films. Scratches, scrapes and screaming tyres would, for once, be acceptable.

The movies were promoted like mainstream cinema releases, with posters, trailer-style TV spots and previews in industry trade magazines like *Variety* and the *Hollywood Reporter*. The first film went online on 25 April 2001. In just nine months, bmwfilms. com had logged more than 10 million film views by 2.13 million people. The agency conducted pre- and post-testing in order to monitor the effectiveness of the campaign. It transpired that those who had seen the films not only emerged with raised perceptions of the performance and handling of a BMW, but also unexpected traits like value for money and safety, which were by no means addressed by 'the driver' on his perilous missions. In other words, the films enhanced the overall image of BMW. Additionally, the agency estimated that, compared to a conventional TV campaign, *The Hire* achieved the same exposure at less than 50 per cent of the cost.

SIZE ISN'T EVERYTHING

Long after the Austin Seven and its licensed German doppelganger had been forgotten, BMW skilfully co-opted another British brand: Mini. The attractive little car was the only good thing to have emerged from BMW's disastrous acquisition of The Rover Group in 1994. For BMW, Mini was a much-loved brand that had been gravely underexploited by its former owners. Putting together a

German and British design team – sparks flew as they fought for their differing visions – the company eventually came up with a contemporary version of the legendary auto. When the feisty new Mini was about to hit American streets in 2002, advertising agency Crispin Porter & Bogusky faced two challenges. The first, the most obvious, was to sell a diminutive European car in a market where size was still important. And the second, underlying mission was to ensure at any cost that the Mini was not classed as a 'chick's car'. The redesigned Beetle had fallen into that trap and, despite its initial success, sales were faltering.

One of Bogusky's first stunts was to park a Mini atop a giant SUV and roll the combo around major cities. Anybody who had tried to park an SUV in the city centre immediately appreciated the joke. The agency also removed a block of seats in a ballpark and placed a Mini in the middle of them, as if the car was settling down to watch the match. In addition, there was a slew of conventional and internet-based advertising, using the British-inflected slogan 'Let's Motor'. A website selling 'Mini motoring gear' was created, reinforcing the idea that the car was more than just a way of getting from A to B: it was a lifestyle choice. BMW let it be known that only a limited volume of Minis would be produced, creating a cult ambience around the vehicle. The campaign was so successful that people camped out in front of dealerships on the night before the first Minis were due to arrive.

A year later, in 2003, Mini repeated a trick it had first played in its Swinging Sixties heyday: it scooped a starring role in a heist movie called *The Italian Job*, an American remake of the 1969 original. Ironically, behind the wheel of the new Mini was Mark Wahlberg, whose almost-naked body had caused such consternation among less physically impressive males in the early 1990s (see Chapter 3). Not too much danger of the Mini being regarded as a conveyance for women, then.

The anxiety lingered, though, right up until the launch of the 2007 Mini Cooper. The solution was an online campaign that plugged straight into thirty-something male fantasies, while displaying the chirpy good-humour for which the Mini brand had become known. Mini's new agency – Butler, Shine, Stern & Partners from California – turned for inspiration to 1970s and 80s TV shows like *The Six Million Dollar Man*, *Magnum* and, more specifically, *Knight Rider*. These series now seemed so thinly plotted, naïve and, frankly, cheesy that they had gained cult appeal among pop culture ironists. Harking back to the success of *The Hire* for BMW, the agency created a six-part online adventure series called *Hammer & Coop*. It featured a macho, moustached driver – Hammer – and his talking Mini Cooper, which inevitably came equipped with a sarcastic English drawl. The four-minute segments, nicknamed 'webisodes', were released over a six-week period on a dedicated website (www.hammerandcoop.com) and on YouTube. In order to promote them, Mini created fake covers featuring Hammer and Coop for the magazines *Rolling Stone* and *Premiere*.

'We wanted to do [the ad campaign] in a way that certainly was more unconventional, more befitting of the Mini brand,' Mini Cooper USA spokesman Andrew Cutler told *The Washington Times*. 'And when you deliver a webisode that's delivered to someone's desktop, you have that one-on-one relationship with them.' ('Crisp pitch with macho cheese: Mini Cooper bypasses TV with retro-look "webisodes"', 1 March 2007.)

The campaign was yet another confirmation that advertisers were worried about the effectiveness of TV advertising. By luring consumers to a branded website, asking them to register their details, and then providing four minutes of funny, self-deprecating entertainment in return, Mini was ensuring that it had their full attention.

That same year, the redesigned Fiat 500 – another motoring legend – also turned to the internet ahead of conventional advertising. During the run-up to the car's launch, a community website called '500 wants you' was established. This encouraged potential buyers to propose design tweaks and get involved in the marketing of the car. In the 'Configuration Lab', visitors could play with the vehicle and choose from a range of colours and accessories, posting the results in a virtual art gallery. Elsewhere on the site, '500ology' was a crowd-sourced encyclopaedia in which participants could add thoughts, comments and stories about the car. A series of video clips featured laddish 'Fiat employees' playing pranks on their bosses. And finally, via the site, members of the public were encouraged to come up with a launch advertising poster for the car, with the help of an array of images and graphics. The campaign had much of the jauntiness of the Mini launch and appealed to young, fashion-conscious consumers. The Fiat 500, in fact, was positioned as a gender-free vehicle – the CK One of motoring.

ROUTES TO THE CONSUMER

Let's not be fooled, though: men are impressed by large and powerful machines. The conventional car advertisement features an automobile, initially shot from above, driven fast along a ribbon of road. Add some spectacular scenery, maybe a special effect or two, and the job is done. Mostly we don't see the driver, but the suggestion of power and forward momentum create a masculine tone. Not all car advertising is this banal – but a surprising amount of it is.

'Scratch a Mini-driving metrosexual and you'll find a man who dreams of fast cars and beautiful women,' claims Genevieve Flaven of Style-Vision. 'Even though automobile manufacturers have softened their approach to advertising, it's difficult to shatter the image of the car as a mirror of masculine power.' Her agency's research has even turned up environmentally-concerned males who cycle to work every day – but keep an SUV parked in their driveways for weekend adventuring. 'The luxury hybrid SUV launched by Lexus has been successful, in my opinion, because it combines environmental friendliness with a muscular body shape.'

Flaven also warns us not to forget motorcycles, possibly the ultimate fusion of man and machine. She notes that 'power biking' has been on the rise in India since the success of the testosterone-fuelled blockbuster *Dhoom* (2004). Motorbike manufacturer Bajaj has seen sales of its Pulsar model increase as a result. 'The Pulsar was launched in 2001 with the slogan, "Definitely Male",' adds Flaven, with a wry smile.

On the four-wheeled front, one of the biggest successes of recent decades has been the Hummer – the giant SUV launched by General Motors in 1992. It is, of course, based on a military vehicle: the High Mobility Multipurpose Wheeled Vehicle, or Humvee. The Hummer looks like unfiltered masculinity, with its stocky tyres, solid frame and military bearing. Indeed, many Hummer owners have made their vehicles available for emergency situations and taken lifesaving courses so they can be of genuine help if needed. Arnold Schwarzenegger is often cited as a Hummer fan, and the brand could wish for no better endorsement.

More recently, however, a vehicle has emerged that wants to out-macho the Hummer. In 2007 Navistar International Corp. signed a US$631 million contract to supply the U.S. Marines with its mine-resistant MaxxPro trucks. Apparently these will phase out Humvees, which proved more vulnerable to mines in Iraq. Navistar quickly announced that it would be taking on the Hummer in civilian life, too, by launching a highway-friendly version of the MaxxPro: 'the humungous, tough-as-nails MXT'. ('Navistar takes aim at Hummer', *Advertising Age*, 9 July 2007.)

As well as negotiating a product placement deal with the HBO surf series *John from Cincinnati*, Navistar and its agency – Fathom Communications – created video clips for YouTube. One of these featured an 'unworthy' man training to get keys to the MXT in a video called 'You are a Champ'. No room for subtlety here: only a real man deserves an MXT.

Sophisticated executives often require a more subtle approach than a direct appeal to their inner warrior. As well as its very male-oriented sponsorship activities – motor racing, golf and sailing – BMW has devised initiatives that create a mystique around its vehicles. One of these is a concept it calls BMW Fine Art. Uwe Ellinghaus explains: 'We have provided a number of luxury hotels with our cars, particularly roadsters and convertibles. These are made available to guests, who can then drive them out for a spin in the countryside. If they want to drive to a restaurant in the evening and enjoy a glass of wine, we provide a chauffeur to bring them back. In this way, we reach potential customers while they're in a receptive mood – and it also solves the problem of convincing time-poor business people to take a test drive.'

With such delightfully unobtrusive techniques at his disposal, why would Ellinghaus still bother with something as basic as television advertising? After all, half the people in front of the box will never be able to afford a BMW – or work for a company that might give them the keys to one. 'I rely on traditional media activity to create desirability around the brand,' Ellinghaus responds. 'It's the "I wish I could afford one" factor. This appeals to some BMW buyers, who get a quiet kick out of making the entire neighbourhood envious when they arrive home in their new car.'

And kids, especially boys, can exert a surprising influence on the purchase decision when they've seen an ad for a car that strikes them as cool.

As we discovered at the beginning, as many women as men own cars. The pleasure of driving is certainly not lost on women. It's fair to assume that there are plenty of female motoring fanatics. But manufacturers and marketers still view the car as an inherently masculine object. And it's impossible to deny the talismanic significance of the automobile in male culture.

BRANDING TOOLKIT

- A fast car remains a metaphor for success, power and control.

- Women are rarely targeted by ad campaigns for cars.

- Auto makers hate it when a model is considered 'a chick's car'.

- But women will buy into an auto brand with a 'masculine' image.

- Leading automobile brands have consistent brand values.

- Web advertising has proved highly effective for car brands.

- Cars are now seeded at luxury hotels for alternative test drives.

6

Travel

Scene Six: On the Move

His morning at the office had gone smoothly. After parking the car he'd walked through Soho, a part of London for which he had a genuine affection, with its human-scaled streets and the hint of village ambience under the carapace of grime. He stopped at a newsagent to buy *The Times*. He had a curious loyalty towards the newspaper – his parents had always read it, and he had followed suit in his teens. But he didn't subscribe because he travelled so often that the deliveries would have ended up forming a dam on his doormat. And besides, he liked the morning flirtation with the girl at the shop.

He scanned the headlines while standing at the counter of Bar Italia, the coffee bar in Frith Street that had barely changed since the fifties. He loved the sepia authenticity of the place, with its huge poster of Rocky Marciano and the cracked leather boxing gloves hanging nearby. The café always seemed alive with energy: the garrulous staff, the harassed motorcycle couriers, the film industry runners checking their watches, the hiss and sputter of the coffee machine. In ten minutes he had downed his ritual espresso and was gone.

The agency was located in a narrow flagstoned courtyard with a single street lamp, slightly askew. He climbed the cramped stairs, tapped in the entry code and passed the deserted reception desk. Dumped the newspaper and bag in his office, roused his Mac, and went straight in to his early morning meeting with Bernard, his boss.

'I won't be doing a hard sell,' he explained. 'It's just an exploratory meeting. They want to see some of our work. I'll do the usual credentials presentation and sound them out a bit.'

This was the Paris meeting, with a family-owned French fashion chain that was expanding overseas. In the last eighteen months they'd opened two shops in Spain and three in Italy. London would follow next year, then Tokyo and New York. But before they went global they wanted a top-to-bottom overhaul of the brand: logo, shop fronts, point of sale material… They'd spoken to a couple of French agencies but they wanted 'an Anglo-Saxon feel'.

Bernard said: 'Well, use your celebrated charm. You know I'd come with you, but I've got the rebranding Swindon meeting this afternoon.'

'I'm sure I'll be fine.'

He'd spent the next couple of hours refining the agency's credentials, selecting past projects that were more relevant to the potential client. At around 11.30 he left the office and walked to the intersection with Oxford Street, where he flagged down a taxi. Inside the vehicle, the radio was tuned to the dance music station Kiss 100. The clattering beat transported him briefly back to a nightclub, circa 1990. He assumed the station knew it had a niche audience of past-it former clubbers.

It was still disorienting to go to the new Eurostar terminal at St Pancras International. It seemed very glitzy compared to Waterloo – more airport-like than ever. There was also a stronger emphasis on retail, with many more opportunities to consume. Posters targeting business travellers hurled advice at him. He'd booked a Business Premium ticket so he passed swiftly through security (such a relief after the airport) and headed straight for the lounge.

Now he's waiting for his train and drinking yet another coffee. He knows it's infantile, but the slick lounge and its freebies give him a secret thrill of elitism. Somebody has left a copy of *The Financial Times* on the table and he flicks idly through it. His eye snags on an ad for Rolex and he wonders whether it's time to trade up. The agency is thriving, Bernard trusts him, and he feels secure. But there's something a bit obvious – a bit *arriviste* – about a Rolex. Even though he's little more than a glorified travelling salesman, he doesn't want to feel like one.

Finally they call his train and he goes through, trundling the Samsonite bag behind him.

MOVING TARGET

Along with young consumers, business travellers are the most enthusiastically hunted prey of marketers. In airports around the world, posters advertise financial services, technology, clothes, watches, pens, aftershave, newspapers and automobiles. Men, particularly, are known to be enthusiastic airport shoppers, as they have time on their hands and are free of the constraints that might prevent them from picking up a tie or a pair of sunglasses during a normal working day. Although not all businessmen are as wealthy as the images projected at them suggest (according to the European Media Survey, they earn an average of €55,000 a year) their aspirational tastes make them desirable targets. The journey from the office to a business meeting abroad resembles a long tunnel of marketing, with many different 'touch points'.

Spafax is an agency specializing in creating 'entertainment and communication experiences' that target frequent travellers – advertising vehicles, in other words. It configures the seat-back in-flight entertainment systems on many aircraft, as well as publishing the glossy magazines in the seat pockets. It has offices in London, California, Singapore and Dubai, among other places (see www.spafax.com). And as senior sales manager Nick Hopkins explains, for advertisers the aeroplane is only half the story.

'We use the journey corridor to create as many touch points as possible. Let's say it's the launch of a car. There will be advertising in the airport. There will be leaflets in the lounge. We've also created Bluetooth opportunities: while you're in the lounge, you receive a message on your mobile asking if you'd like to download details of the car. And all this activity is pushing you to a micro-site on the in-flight entertainment system.'

Other possibilities for clients include sponsorship options, such as providing PCs, printers or cell phone chargers in lounges. Food and beverage companies have been known to offer customers in-flight samples.

'Frequent flyers are upscale, sophisticated consumers,' observes Hopkins. 'So your marketing material should enhance their travel experience. Airlines used to be very protective, particularly concerning the VIP lounge, but gradually they are seeing the benefit of partnering with premium brands.'

Once on board the plane, many frequent flyers demand cutting edge entertainment systems. Hopkins says, 'Ten years ago, business travellers would spend most of the flight tapping away on their laptops. Now, they fold their computers away and relax quite soon into the flight. I think business people are so bombarded with work-related messages that they view the aircraft as a haven. It may be their only opportunity to relax that week.'

According to the Inflight Management Development Centre (IMDC), airlines will spend US$12.9 billion keeping their customers amused between 2006 and 2011. Seat-back entertainment systems now typically offer a dazzling array of the very latest movies alongside news, TV shows, sport, documentaries, music, and video games. A report by Mintel notes: 'Noise cancelling headsets, the ability to pause, rewind, fast forward and repeat both music and video, interactive video games, moving maps, live TV and news broadcasts are all features addressing the multi-channel and internet-led "dip in, dip out" mentality of today's consumers.' (Onboard Entertainment, UK, May 2007.)

'It was much easier for us when we only had to provide two or three movies on our systems,' admits Hopkins. 'But now we have to offer the latest blockbusters, as well as independent films. Our in-flight systems are so good that people rarely bring portable DVD players on board. Why would they, when they can see a film that's just hit cinema screens?'

All this has made in-flight advertising more sophisticated too. In the past, typical media placements would have included meal tray cards, seatbacks and a commercial or two on the entertainment system. But digital media has provided new opportunities. Interactive systems have made the experience more immersive, which translates into a more engaged passenger for advertisers. For example, the systems can serve up interactive brochures. Touch the screen to see your dream car revolve 360 degrees, and then touch again to change its colour. And because they are digital, these systems can store more data about what the passenger is watching, for how long. Once connected to the internet, passengers will be able to book a test drive while they're still in the air: the car will be waiting for them at the airport.

In-flight media also present plenty of opportunities for more traditional advertising. For instance, British cinema sales house Pearl & Dean – which usually sells advertising slots in movie theatres – has added its service to in-flight entertainment on Virgin

Atlantic. As British audiences are used to experiencing the firm's logo and jingle in cinemas, followed by some of that month's best advertising, they happily accept it in this new environment.

Now plans are afoot to merge in-flight entertainment systems with the frequent traveller's own portable technology. Wireless internet, iPod docking and mobile phone connectivity were all on the cards at the time of writing.

Even the humble in-flight magazine has gone hip. More than 60 different titles are published worldwide, and the ads they contain bring in extra revenue for airlines. 'They used to be bland and generic,' says Hopkins. 'But frequent travellers have very specific needs. They love to read about sport, business, gadgets and travel. More than that, the magazine should act as a guide to their destination, informing them about everything that will be going on when they hit the ground. It has to be more relevant than a regular magazine.'

THE SEDUCTION OF SLEEP

Of course, it's not just the entertainment system that is more elaborate in business class. Airlines lure frequent travellers with increased personal space and comfortable seats that stretch out into beds, as well as the snobbish satisfaction of knowing that less fortunate passengers have been screened off with a contemptuous flick of a curtain.

The widely admired – and imitated – British Airways Club World began the 'battle of the beds' when it installed the first entirely reclining seat in 2000. This was by no means the limit of the amenities on offer. The Club World traveller could expect arrivals lounges equipped with gyms, showers, dry cleaning and hot breakfasts, pre-flight dining in the departure lounge, extensive menus and wine lists onboard the aircraft, hours of in-flight entertainment, plus highly attentive service. Economy class passengers who found themselves in Club World might have felt as though they'd plunged into a parallel universe in which air travel was actually pleasurable.

The more recent emergence of a 'premium economy' category aimed at leisure travellers – placed midway between the luxury of business and the grimness of economy – has made it imperative that the executive service appears even more extravagant than before. In 2007 British Airways announced that it had spent US$200 million upgrading Club World, putting some air between itself and other brands that had imitated its offering. The new amenities included an in-flight buffet stocked with food and drink, a touch-operated privacy screen and a seat that was 25 per cent wider. It was probably the latter that customers noticed the most, because research shows that business travellers prize one thing above all else on long-haul flights, and that is sleep.

Seasoned travellers knock back a couple of glasses of wine with the pre-flight meal in the lounge, and once inside the aircraft are ready to flatten their seats almost as soon as the fasten seatbelts sign has been extinguished. British Airways played on this brilliantly in a 2003 advertisement. It showed a businessman climbing into bed in Times Square, and waking fully refreshed in Piccadilly Circus. The ad struck a chord with all those who had tried to make it through a crucial meeting straight off a flight from New York. Many other airlines, from Singapore to Lufthansa, have used the promise of sleep – or personal space – as a marketing tool.

Frequent flyers complain about the rigours of travel, but racking up air miles is also a source of secret pride for many men. Like working late at the office or finishing a task over the weekend, jetting around the world on the company makes them feel industrious, relevant and ever so slightly glamorous. An article in *The Sunday Times* described 'extreme jobs' as those in which people work 'more than 60 hours a week, travel widely and are under plenty of performance pressure'. The paper described this manic lifestyle as 'the business equivalent of bungee jumping'.

Sylvia Ann Hewlett, a professor at Columbia University in New York, warned that it was 'dangerously alluring'. After spending a year studying high-earning professionals – mostly men – she concluded that they loved their jobs, even though 'the fallout is wreaking havoc in [their] private lives'. Half of them, she noted, didn't have sex any more because they were too exhausted. ('70 hours a week to get to the top', 4 February 2007.)

The article went on to quote the 37-year-old managing partner of a law firm in Manchester, who reckoned he worked a 70-hour week. 'I'm an M&A [mergers and acquisitions] lawyer, so if I have a large transaction and am working to deadline, I can work two or three days without sleep. I don't drink at all, and I take lots of Red Bull [energy drink]… I love the work and the opportunities this job gives me. Where else can you earn very good money, meet lots of people and have a very social job? I can be in London one day, Manchester another day, flying over to Europe another.'

He admitted that he found it impossible to keep still, rarely settling down to watch TV or read a book. 'I wake up at 6am and am out of the house at 6.30am. I run in the evenings or during the day… Always being on the go is a result of being very ambitious and very competitive. Being in business is the biggest competition you can be involved in and the most fascinating. You're competing against a lot of people and… it's the most motivating contest you can be in.'

Advertising may have moved on from the hyper-committed executive figure it often used in 1980s commercials, but the real deal is still out there, competing with his fellow males by racking up longer hours and more flights, scoring points by packing light and being the first out of the terminal into a taxi.

ATTACKING MR JETSET

In Europe, many travellers are beginning to ask themselves whether flying is really the most efficient solution. Security phobia has turned most airports into Kafkaesque labyrinths, with Heathrow topping the list of travellers' least-loved hubs. Interminable check-ins, brusque security staff, the indignity of forced shoe removal and the injudiciously applied liquid ban are all encouraging consumers to snub airports – at least for short-haul destinations.

The alternative is Europe's growing network of high-speed rail services. With tickets growing more affordable and technology advancing apace – trains now travel at up to 330 km/h – gliding is becoming hipper than flying. In July 2007, seven of Europe's high-speed train operators formed an alliance called RailTeam, whose goal is to offer seamless rail transport across the continent (www.railteam.eu). At the time of writing, the service links France with the UK, Holland, Belgium, Switzerland, Germany and Austria. By 2010 it expects to carry 25 million customers and serve 65 cities. It is estimated that actual travel now accounts for 20 per cent of the flying experience, so for trips of a short to moderate length, the train makes more sense. With security kept to a minimum, business travellers can use the time they would have spent in a queue tapping away at their laptops while verdant countryside zips past their window.

One of the main brands to benefit from this rail revolution is Eurostar, which in November 2007 opened its new terminal at St Pancras International. The station served a newly-operational stretch of high speed rail line that cut journey times between London and Paris to two hours and fifteen minutes – and between London and Brussels to just over an hour and fifty minutes.

Eurostar UK marketing director Greg Nugent can list numerous reasons why the train is better than the plane, concern over climate change being one of them. 'Business people are well-informed and the debate about emissions certainly won't have escaped them. Many will opt for the train to reduce their carbon footprint, perhaps at the prompting of their employers. In general, though, they just hate being seen as out of date.'

Eurostar has created a programme called Tread Lightly, which aims to reduce carbon emissions by 25 per cent per customer by 2012. But this is by no means the first time the rail service has attacked air travel.

In 2002, it embarked on an initiative to 'relaunch' the Eurostar brand with a campaign that directly targeted business travellers. At the time, there were already several factors in Eurostar's favour. The business world was tightening its belt after 9/11, with restrictions on travel expenditure. The image of flying was still wobbly, with residual paranoia about possible terrorist attacks. Eurostar was seen as relatively stress- and hassle-free compared to flying, and punctuality was at an all-time high – an obvious plus for the business community.

At the same time, however, Eurostar was being forced to compete with low-cost airlines. Many business travellers were locked into frequent flyer programmes that delivered air miles. Worse than that, they considered Eurostar 'basic and functional' compared to the VIP service they were used to getting on long-haul business travel. Overseas trips were so linked to the executive lifestyle that some passengers felt that flying conferred status – to fly for work was to have arrived. ('Eurostar – How Mr JetSet made Eurostar mean business', IPA Effectiveness Awards, 2006.)

Greg Nugent recalls: 'When I came to work at Eurostar, it had very little experience in targeting business travellers. I felt they shouldn't be too much of a problem to reach because they were easy to spot and had obvious needs. We worked with a psychologist called John Armstrong to identify exactly what they got out of flying. Among several insights, we found that they felt flying on business gave them some sort of elite status, while secretly admitting that it was boring and stressful.'

Business travellers demand special treatment. They do not like to be associated with tourists – in fact, they like to remain as far away from the herd as possible – and they demand certain comforts that help them work more efficiently either during or at the other end of their journey. But Nugent and his team unearthed another insight, which is that business travellers are not *just* business travellers.

'Looking at a crop of advertising campaigns at the time, we realized that business people were essentially being treated like idiots. They were all lumped into this Wall Street, hard-nosed executive category and they were expected to blindly buy into that. It was always the guy sitting on a plane in his shirt and tie being served a glass of champagne, or punching the air after sealing a deal.'

Internally, this character was referred to as 'Lufthansa Man'. He later morphed into 'Mr JetSet'.

'We wanted to target the intelligent business traveller. After all, business people are just people. Yes, many of them will work on their way to a meeting – but often, on the way home, they've loosened their ties and are getting stuck in to a good book, or a magazine, or a DVD. They're not the one-dimensional work machines you see in most of the advertising aimed at them. We felt that somebody like David Brent [the clueless boss in the TV series *The Office*] would take the plane just because he thought it was cool. But the more informed traveller would opt for the train.'

Eurostar wanted to build a reputation around its business service, which includes stylish lounges, efficient online booking and a frequent travellers' programme. Nugent adds: 'We worked on getting the experience right first, because if we'd just relied on the media, the campaign would not have succeeded. There has to be a very strong element of word-of-mouth.'

Nevertheless, the print advertising campaign devised by Eurostar and its agency TBWA London was a key element. It featured an obnoxious cartoon character called Mr JetSet, who retained his fixed grin and self-satisfied demeanour despite the privations of flying. His catchphrase was, 'I came by plane, you know.' Other captions included: 'With no space for his laptop, Mr JetSet can demonstrate his mental agility'; and '35 missed calls only prove to Mr JetSet how important he is.' A closed check-in gave Mr JetSet ample opportunity to bellow about how crucial it was that he made his meeting. Each of the posters asked: 'Fed up with flying? Fly Eurostar.'

In this way, the business traveller was practically shamed into choosing the train instead of the plane for reaching Paris or Brussels. Eurostar saw a subsequent sharp increase in the sales of business class tickets.

While airlines are clearly safe from the challenge of rail on most routes, high speed trains are now criss-crossing Europe – just as bullet trains are streaking across Japan, China and South Korea. The United States has long languished behind – but airport misery, rising petrol prices and traffic congestion have brought the issue to the fore. The wait on the platform could be lengthy, however. 'U.S. passenger trains chug along at little more than highway speeds – slowed by a half-century of federal preference for spending on roads and airports,' moaned *The Chicago Sun-Times*. It observed that although Congress is considering a six-year Amtrak funding bill, the measure proposes US$100 million in first-year grants, 'paltry considering that California alone needs US$40 billion for a mammoth bullet train project that would link San Francisco and Sacramento with Los Angeles and San Diego' ('Still on training wheels', 7 September 2007).

In the United States and around the world, Mr JetSet will remain a familiar figure in the well-appointed executive lounges that are his natural habitat. But the Eurostar experience in the UK demonstrates that he is developing a conscience – and that marketing to him requires more imagination than it did in the past.

BRANDING TOOLKIT

- Business travellers are enthusiastic airport shoppers.

- They expect a luxurious travel experience.

- This includes sophisticated in-flight entertainment.

- In-flight marketing initiatives should add to their experience.

- Sleep, privacy and legroom remain important marketing tools.

- Frequent flyers are becoming concerned about their 'carbon footprint'.

- In Europe and parts of Asia, the train is threatening the plane.

- Business people are tiring of the 'inhumanity' of air travel.

The bachelor pad of the future may look like this,
according to Philips.

YOUR DAD WAS NOT A METROSEXUAL

He didn't do pilates. Moisturize. Or drink pink cocktails. Your Dad drank whisky cocktails. Made with Canadian Club. Served in a rocks glass. They tasted good. They were effortless. **DAMN RIGHT YOUR DAD DRANK IT**

Canadian Club® Blended Canadian Whisky, 40% Alc./Vol. ©2007 Canadian Club Import Company, Deerfield, IL

Canadian Club.

This campaign for Canadian Club suggests a metrosexual backlash.

YOUR MOM WASN'T YOUR DAD'S FIRST

He went out. He got two numbers in the same night. He drank cocktails. But they were whisky cocktails. Made with Canadian Club. Served in a rocks glass. They tasted good. They were effortless. **DAMN RIGHT YOUR DAD DRANK IT**

Canadian Club.

(Image courtesy of Energy BBDO)

Dunhill creates a masculine lifestyle experience.

The interior of one of Dunhill's 'homes' suggests a gentlemen's club of the old school.

*Return of the dandy? Savile Row clothing brand Gieves & Hawkes
has benefited from a resurgence of interest in classic styles.*

(Image courtesy of Gieves & Hawkes)

(Image courtesy of Gieves & Hawkes)

'The average age of our customer has dropped by more than ten years' – Mark Henderson, Gieves & Hawkes.

BMW: an automobile company that is also a lifestyle brand.

Stunts like this helped the diminutive Mini find a niche in a market of giant cars.

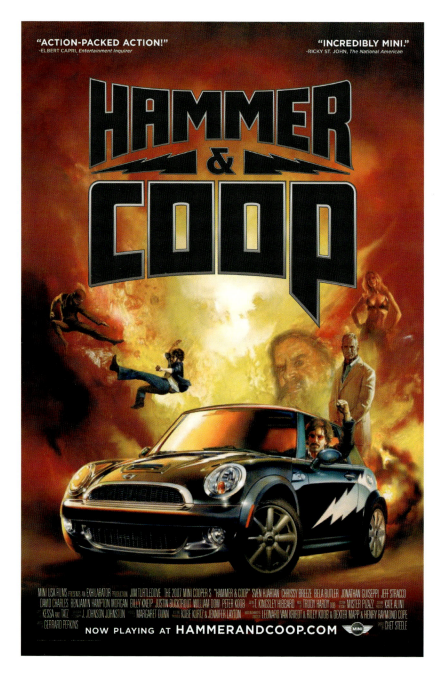

Ironic machismo underlines the notion that Mini is not a 'chick's car'.

Guinness has scored with intelligent male drinkers thanks to its consistently sharp and amusing advertising.

(Images courtesy of Diageo)

(Images courtesy of Diageo)

Smirnoff plays on the dramatic history of the brand to capture the imaginations of consumers.

(Images courtesy of Diageo)

Words

He stops fussing with the credentials presentation and stows his laptop. It's going to be a long day and he reckons he deserves a break. In his bag he's packed the latest Michael Connelly thriller and the UK edition of the magazine *Esquire*, which he picked up with his newspaper that morning. He doesn't feel like concentrating on the convoluted plot of the novel, so he decides to flick through the magazine before lunch. It's toned down the tits-and-ass recently and he feels marginally less self-conscious about reading it. Apart from that, the publication enables him to slyly monitor what the well-dressed man about town is supposed to be wearing these days.

He reckons he was in at the birth of men's magazines in Britain. When he was in his early teens, the only way to look at the new Porsche one minute and beautiful girls the next was to have the motoring supplement of *The Sunday Times* open next to his mother's *Vogue*. That was until some time around his 15th birthday, in 1986, and the launch of a magazine called *Arena*. Finally, here was a publication that covered clothes, girls and cars in equal measure. A British edition of *GQ* followed a little later. He realized that these magazines were too old for him – with their articles about flash threads, fast women and overpriced restaurants – but he aspired. While beyond the doors of his school Thatcher's Britain scrambled for cash, he dreamed of becoming a City trader.

By the time he'd left university, he'd developed a pub habit and a rougher edge. The perfect New Man embodied by *Arena* didn't fit the reality of his hard-working, hard-playing days and nights. That was when a magazine called *Loaded* came along, 'for men who should know better'. Its vulgar, knockabout humour and unabashed anti-feminism made it a guilty pleasure. It was a magazine for 'lads' and for a while that was how he thought of himself. Other men agreed, because before long the entire publishing industry appeared to be targeting this 'new' market of unselfconscious, football-loving males.

As he entered his thirties, he sloughed off that image. His personal and professional pride required that he maintained a broad knowledge of business and current affairs. He spent more time reading newspapers and trade publications, as well as dense marketing tomes. He still bought *GQ* and *Esquire* now and then for the fashion – and, to be honest, the women – but the covers embarrassed him a little. For a while he switched to the US editions, which seemed a little less prurient.

Now in his mid-thirties, he worries about becoming out of touch, so he pays a little more attention to the style press. And he's pleased to see that the magazines at last seem to be growing up with him. *Esquire* is the latest to move upmarket, and he's keen to see how much it has really changed.

GLOSSIES FOR GUYS

Men's magazines have always followed their readers rather than leading them. It's the major difference between the women's glossies and their masculine counterparts – and one that has its roots in the past. Most women could only daydream about the unattainable lives led by the legendary editors of *Vogue* and *Elle* – people like Diana Vreeland and Carmel Snow – who seemed to exist in a perpetual Riviera cocktail party. But the readers of men's magazines frequently earned more money, and had more powerful jobs, than the people who were writing for them. It's unlikely that a well-tailored financier considered a journalist his better. And so the relationship became clubby and conspiratorial. Women's magazines have a tendency to dictate – men's publications advise, banter and flatter.

Due to the far greater size of the market, style magazines for men have always been more self-confident in the United States than in the UK. Three of the most famous brands have intertwined histories – *Esquire*, *Playboy* and *GQ*.

Esquire was launched in the depths of the Depression, on 15 October 1933. It was a spin-off from the trade publication *Apparel Arts*, published by David A. Smart, William H. Weintraub and Arnold Gingrich. The trio had been getting reports that their industry journal was so handsome that customers often asked if they could take it home with them. Clearly there was a market for a consumer magazine about men's style. The original plan was that *Esquire* (which cost 50 cents) would be sold mostly through men's outfitters. Of the first print run of 95,000, only 5,000 were placed on newsstands. These sold out almost immediately, and the publishers scrabbled to recover some of the copies they had reserved for stores and rush them to the kiosks. *Esquire* established the template for a mid-century masculine title, with a combination of men's fashions, meaty fiction – stories by Hemingway and F. Scott Fitzgerald – and pin-ups in the form of the Varga Girls: voluptuous pulp fiction-esque sirens from the imagination of illustrator Alberto Vargas.

This blend of style, intellect and titillation has survived more-or-less intact down the years – although the measures have varied wildly. One only has to look at the satirical cover designs of art director George Lois in the 1960s (www.georgelois.com) to see how far the bar has been lowered since then. But *Esquire* remains a powerful international media brand, with over a dozen editions worldwide.

In its early years, *Esquire* was based in Chicago. On its staff was a young advertising copywriter named Hugh Hefner. When the magazine relocated to New York, Hefner demanded a pay rise. His request was turned down, so he decided to stay behind and launch his own publication. As he struggled to scrape a living with other publishers (including a stint as circulation manager for *Children's Activities* magazine) he refined a concept for a risqué but debonair magazine for men. The first issue of *Playboy* was blocked out on Hefner's kitchen table in 1953. The debut issue contained nude pictures of Marilyn Monroe – purchased from the local printer of a calendar – a Sherlock Holmes short story and an article about modern office design. It sold a respectable 51,000 copies – enough to justify a second issue. For many years, *Playboy* was as much about words as it was about pictures, offering short stories by Arthur C. Clarke, Alberto Moravia and William Styron, among others. Hef once told a group of his 'Playmate' models, 'If it wasn't for you, I'd be running a literary magazine.' But competition from men's style magazines in the 1980s forced *Playboy* to place more of an emphasis on flesh.

Meanwhile, in 1958, the publishers of *Apparel Arts* had re-launched their trade journal as a quarterly fashion supplement to *Esquire*. The new publication concentrated solely on clothing and was called *Gentlemen's Quarterly*. It remained part of the *Esquire* stable until 1983, when it was sold to *Vogue* publisher Condé Nast – who renamed it *GQ*.

Around the time that *Gentlemen's Quarterly* was founded, a young man named Arthur Cooper – who was to have a considerable impact on the magazine's future – was graduating from Pennsylvania State University. Art Cooper went on to work as a political correspondent for the *Patriot-News* in Harrisburg, followed by stints at *Time* magazine and *Newsweek*. At the latter post, he was interviewed for the job of features editor at *Playboy*. His five-page memo about how the magazine could be made more relevant to a 1970s readership was rejected, and he didn't get the job. Undeterred, he expanded the memo to 30 pages and sent it to Bob Guccione, the founder and editor of rival publication *Penthouse*. Guccioni not only appreciated the advice, he hired Art as editor-in-chief.

Like the readers of top-shelf magazines who claim they 'enjoy the articles', Cooper said that he was not interested in the cruder side of *Penthouse*. 'Whatever Bob was doing upstairs was a separate thing. I had nothing to do with the pictures.' ('He changed the face of men's magazines, with Sinatra as his model', *The Guardian*, 11 June 2003.)

Paradoxically, Cooper's next job was as editor of *Family Weekly*, where he continued publishing quality fiction alongside core content. In 1983 he got the call he'd been hoping for – Condé Nast wanted him to edit the stylish newcomer to its stable, *GQ*. A larger-than-life figure, Art was perfect for the role. 'Cooper came to embody the GQ Man,' comments *The Guardian*. 'In the 1980s, he wore striped shirts with polka dot ties, starting a trend in the fashion world. In the 1990s it was mostly black cashmere turtlenecks with grey or black sport coats.'

At the time of Cooper's appointment, many straight men had the lingering suspicion that *GQ* was aimed mainly at a gay readership. Cooper took it mainstream by retaining the focus on fashion, but leavening it with material that reflected his own interests: literature, food, investigative reporting and sports. Under his editorship, its readership overtook that of *Esquire*, and circulation rose from 565,000 to more than 850,000. Cooper edited the magazine for 20 years, dying of a heart attack a few months after his retirement in 2003. In his obituary, *The Guardian* commented: 'The magazine... had an impact which extended beyond New York, indeed beyond the United States. *GQ* set a style for the first part of a new wave of men's magazines that swept across

Western Europe and the industrialized world in the late 1980s and 1990s.'

FROM SMOOTH OPERATORS TO NEW LADS

Nonetheless, men's magazines had existed, on and off, for a very long time in the United Kingdom. The splendidly comprehensive Magforum.com offers a full rundown. Careful scrutiny suggests that 'the first modern magazine' was called *The Gentleman's Magazine*, published by one Edward Cave in 1731 under the name 'Sylvanus Urban'. In his famous dictionary, Doctor Samuel Johnson – who actually penned articles for the publication – credits Cave as the originator of the term 'magazine' in the publishing sense: previously it meant storehouse or arsenal. According to Magforum.com, *The Gentleman's Magazine* survived until 1914 when 'like many other titles in the UK, it was killed off by the advent of the Great War'.

Another pioneering publication was *Man About Town*, which Magforum describes as 'the first modern consumer style magazine for men'. Interestingly, its beginnings resemble those of *Esquire* – and of a later publication called *For Him*, which we'll discuss shortly. The magazine was launched as a quarterly in 1952 by John Taylor, editor of the trade journal *Tailor & Cutter* and apparently something of a raconteur. 'For Taylor, *Man About Town* was the perfect platform to indulge his interests in fine wines – especially champagne – good food, women and entertaining company.' It sounds like an appealing mixture, and indeed *Man About Town* became a cult hit. The magazine was sold to a company called Cornmarket (today's Haymarket Media Group) in 1960. Its name was abbreviated to *About Town* and finally *Town*.

Under this truncated appendage, *Town*, along with its women's counterparts *Queen* and *Nova*, had its heyday in the Swinging Sixties. However, for all these titles, attracting advertising was always a challenge, especially with the advent of newspaper colour supplements. By the late 1960s, *Town* couldn't stand the competition for advertising cash, and – like the legendary women's fashion monthly *Nova* – closed in 1967; *Queen* was merged into US title *Harper's Bazaar* to become *Harper's and Queen*.

There were many other non-pornographic men's titles that thrived through the first half of the 20th century, but the advent of television robbed them of advertising and they faltered in the late 1950s and 1960s, usually to be taken over by top-shelf publishers. *Men Only*, for example, which started out as a generalist publication in the thirties, ended up as part of nightclub mogul Paul Raymond's 'adult magazine' empire.

Tony Quinn, the founder of Magforum.com and an expert on the history of British magazine publishing, comments, 'Men's magazines have struggled in the UK for purely commercial reasons. The US market is five times bigger in terms of overall population, and 10 times bigger in terms of sales. From the 1930s through to the 50s there were many popular, pocket-sized British magazines – such as *London Opinion, London Life, Razzle, Men Only* and *Lilliput* – that sold in their hundreds of thousands. Just before the war, new colour printing presses were installed at Watford, providing quality that still looks glorious today. But the war killed off their potential with the rationing of paper and ink. All these men's titles had been established in a pocket format and were unable to make the transition to larger formats when they lost advertising to television and newspaper colour supplements. The likes of *Town, King* and *Club* thrived for a few years in the 1960s, but all succumbed. This inability to compete for advertising also saw off US publishers, which attempted to launch *Esquire* in the UK [in 1953], as well as *Men in Vogue* and *Cosmopolitan Man*. You can easily see why men's magazines practically died out.'

By the 1980s, all the big publishers in Britain felt that there was no market for men's magazines in the UK below the top shelf.

Then, almost out of nowhere, *Arena* appeared. The magazine was the brainchild of Nick Logan, creator of 'style bible' *The Face*. Logan felt that many readers had already grown out of *The Face*, so his new magazine was designed to appeal to them. One of his major assets was the designer Neville Brody, whose work for *The Face* had referenced punk, Dada and architectural influences. Writing in *The Guardian* on the 20th anniversary of *Arena*'s launch, Logan recalled: 'They said it couldn't be done: a magazine for men that was neither top-shelf nor specialist. They'd said something similar about *The Face*. I'd been publishing/editing it for six years when the idea for *Arena* started to form in my mind' ('I taught men to turn over a new page', 24 September 2006).

The title, wrote Logan, was inspired by the mix of fashion and sport in an Italian publication, *Uomo Vogue Sport*, 'less for the action than the ritual, equipment and clothing'. One of the most important British menswear designers also had an unwitting hand in the project. 'I had ringing in my head a comment from Paul Smith – "What do I have to do to get in *The Face*?" – inviting me to think what kind of publication could tap more directly into that designer's increasingly influential sensibility.' Although Logan had a vague 'folk memory' of *Man About Town*, he admits that there was little else to base the magazine on. He envisaged the publication as 'intelligent, hip, with a boldly international outlook, though recognizably, and proudly, British; it would have fashion, art, design, fiction maybe – in appearance it would be faintly old-fashioned, but "of the moment" in attitude and content. And it went without saying it would be a second design landmark for Brody'.

The undeniably cool magazine launched from the exaggerated shoulder pads of Thatcher's Britain and enjoyed a soft landing in an emerging market of aspiring male consumers. The success of *Arena* – whose circulation had reached almost 70,000 two years later – paved the way for the arrival of the British editions of *GQ*, in 1989, and *Esquire*, which finally made it across the Atlantic in 1991 – almost four decades after its original, failed attempt.

Unbeknown to them, a young man called James Brown, who had been a contributor to *Arena*, was about to change the game completely. In May 1994, Brown became the launch editor of a new magazine called *Loaded*, from publisher IPC. Throwing out the steely *froideur* of *Arena*, Brown's magazine was designed to appeal to 'normal blokes' who were interested in 'sex, drink, football and less serious matters'. A bit stubbly and with an incipient beer belly, the *Loaded* reader may have been interested in fashion – but only to show off on the terraces, in the clubs or on the pull. Nevertheless, he wasn't entirely stupid: *Loaded* bloke read lurid tabloid newspapers in a spirit of fun, not because he was incapable of deciphering long sentences. The key to the magazine's success was its accessibility. Everybody could identify with this lifestyle, which was by no means the case with the yuppie manifestos. Nine issues later, *Loaded* was selling around 100,000 copies.

Hot on its sneaker-shod heels was *FHM*, formerly known as *For Him*. The publisher Emap had acquired the title from a small outfit called Tayvale, which had distributed the magazine through men's clothing retailers – much like *Esquire* and *GQ* in the long-ago United States. Emap revamped the title and effectively beat *Loaded* at its own game by closing the gap between journalists and readers. The title's mission statement was 'funny, sexy and useful', with the accent on the latter. Each activity featured in the magazine had to be fully accessible to readers, with full contact details provided so they could have a go themselves.

Not only that, but *FHM* seemed fully at home with the idea that sex sold. At first, men's magazines featured rugged male icons on their covers for fear of being lumped in with top-shelf magazines. But soon the competition between *FHM* and *Loaded* boiled down to which of them could put the hottest babe on the cover – with the other men's titles gleefully following suit. The sex content of all male titles increased, in parallel with a sector-wide shift downmarket. Recalling the era, Kira Cochrane – the women's editor of *The Guardian* – wrote: 'Within months of *Loaded*'s launch, *GQ* had scrapped its "no naked covers" policy, and within a few years it was featuring a female columnist who recounted her first experience of anal sex – something she had done, she wrote, simply because her editor had told her to' ('The dark world of lads' mags', *New Statesman*, 23 August 2007). For Cochrane, lad culture was simply 'old-style sexism dressed up as the new-style irony'.

The sales of *FHM* soon rocketed past those of *Loaded*, rising to 775,000 in the UK by the end of 1999. As they awkwardly tried to remain upmarket while scrambling for a slice of the flesh-fuelled action, *GQ*, *Arena* and *Esquire* alienated both readerships and were left behind in the dust.

The media was now full of talk of a character called 'New Lad' – essentially a fashionably-dressed, smart-mouthed rough diamond. Mark Simpson – the chronicler of the rise of 'metrosexuality' (see Introduction) – comments: 'Supposedly a "backlash" against New Man, [New Lad] was just a much more successful form of metrosexuality: one that millions of men bought... New Lad finally achieved the marketing mother-lode: high-end vanity and fashion advertising delivered to a mass market of young men, for the first time ever. But it was *FHM* that really perfected New Lad, because unlike (the rather middle-class) *Loaded* they weren't embarrassed by fashion and clobber – or male models. In fact, the magazines were really shopping brochures with some editorial about how to light your farts and give women multiple orgasms with your big toe.'

Half a dozen titles launched to target this character – but they all slid the key under the door within a few years. The exception was *Maxim*, launched by Felix Dennis in 1995. (Early in his career Dennis was one of the names behind *Oz*, the sixties counter-culture magazine that provoked an obscenity trial.) Although *Maxim* could not topple *FHM* in the UK, it is noteworthy for having exported the 'New Lad' to the United States in 1997.

The existing high-brow magazines greeted the US edition of *Maxim* with disapproval: Art Cooper wondered aloud why lads' mags carried so much condom advertising when 'their readers are all masturbators' ('Bright lights, big titties', Salon.com, 1 October 1999). Potential American readers were undaunted by this insult: sales of *Maxim* climbed to more than a million, trouncing the haughty *GQ* and *Esquire*. 'The great thing is that it's English journalism and panache,' Felix later claimed. 'Personally, if I wanted to be successful in only one territory that would be America' ('Beating the big boys at their own game', *The Guardian*, 15 August 2005).

Soon *FHM* followed *Maxim* into the United States, and the scene was set for the globalization of the New Lad. Editions of the two magazines began cropping up around the world. By the turn of the millennium, however, there were already signs that the market was reaching maturity. But British publishers remained so enamoured of the format that they launched weekly versions of the 'girls and gadgets' titles, with names like *Zoo* and *Nuts*. It transpired that the weeklies were the last gasp of the New Lad trend.

CLIMBING BACK UPMARKET

It was almost as if a mysterious blight had crept into the roots of lad culture. Abruptly, sales of men's magazines on both sides of the Atlantic began to wither. Figures released in the UK by the Audit Bureau of Circulation in February 2007 showed that sales for the sector had fallen by 14.4 per cent, 'while *FHM*, the market-leading monthly publication, lost 26 per cent... The monthly titles *Loaded*, *Maxim* and *Arena* all lost almost a third of their sales' ('Sales blow for men's magazine market', *Financial Times*, 16 February 2007). One buyer of advertising space described the format as 'tired'. By the autumn of that year, the circulation of *Loaded*, the granddaddy of lads' mags, had declined by almost 30 per cent. Mark Simpson says: 'Having done their job, helping to metrosexualize a generation, the era of men's glossies seems to be drawing to a close. I don't think that today's young males need to be persuaded to go shopping or use vanity products.'

The other cause of the circulation droop was easy to determine – it was the internet. The lads' magazines had occasionally been categorized as porn for cowards, and now those who sought bare flesh had an easy and discreet medium at their, um, fingertips. So, too, did the advertisers hunting them. Adrift and casting around for inspiration, the men's magazines suddenly noticed a hovering group of older, alienated readers who might still be in the market for fashion tips, intelligent writing and flirtations with A-list actresses.

In the United States, this sophisticated older male was already being courted by the extension of an established brand: *Men's Vogue*. While some media buyers remained sceptical about the magazine's appeal ('*Vogue* is a women's brand', sniffed one), editor Jay Fielden had taken a step in the right direction by pledging to put 'real men' – news anchors, explorers, sportsmen – on the fashion pages instead of male models. He understood that American men were uncomfortable with the very idea of 'fashion'. Instead, they merely wanted to 'look good' ('Men's magazines turn the page on their adolescence', *Financial Times*, 26 August 2007). One edition featured former British Prime Minister Tony Blair on the cover – the very antithesis of floozification.

The titles best-placed to take advantage of the move to maturity were the original glossies: *GQ* and *Esquire*. The American edition of *GQ* had never really dumbed down. It had merely been shaken up and modernized after the departure of Art Cooper – although the result was a rather soulless affair, as if Sinatra had been remixed by an electro band. Even the British edition had recovered its poise under its editor Dylan Jones, who understood that it should provide a route out of lad-land. The Brit version of *Esquire* needed attention, however. Its re-launch in August 2007 seemed to draw a line under the era of the lad. New editor Jeremy Langmead promised intelligent writing and 'no B-list floozies'.

His strategy would be to treat the publication as a niche, luxury brand. 'We want the right readers, not lots of wrong ones,' he said ('Jeremy Langmead on the *Esquire* relaunch', *Press Gazette*, 10 August 2007).

Luxury fashion brands seeking upmarket male consumers were wavering about the wisdom of lowering themselves to advertise on the internet, so glossy magazines were still an attractive option. The packaging, though, had to be right. As Langmead implied, for maximum effectiveness the ads of an Armani or a Hugo Boss required a gilded frame, not a couple of blobs of Blutack and a space next to a girlie calendar.

Langmead added: 'I thought what was missing on the newsstand was a magazine for intelligent and sophisticated men, which is what I tried to do. When I was doing research for this, I looked and there was not a magazine I wanted to buy that was both entertaining and informative.'

Men's magazines had gone full circle.

MEN AND NEWSPAPERS

Men may have a somewhat tentative relationship with glossy magazines, but they remain committed to newspapers – whether offline or on. In fact, the International Newspaper Marketing Association released a study in 2003 documenting a continuing slide in newspaper readership among women. 'Exploring the Newspaper Readership Gender Gap' demonstrated that, around the world, women read newspapers less frequently than men – despite the narrowing divide between their incomes and career roles.

A look at newspaper readership on both sides of the Atlantic confirms this claim. In the United Kingdom, the readership of every 'quality' daily newspaper skews male: 57 per cent of the readers of *The Times* and *The Guardian* are male. At *The Independent* the difference is even more marked, with a 61 per cent male readership. Only the mid-market tabloid *The Daily Mail*, which has deliberately targeted women since the beginning – it was the first British newspaper to start a women's page – turns the trend on its head, delivering a 52 per cent female readership (National Readership Survey, January–December 2006). In the United States, the Newspaper Association of America says that 55 per cent of single-copy newspaper buyers are male (NAA Facts about Newspapers, 2004). Official figures provided to advertisers by *The New York Times* confirm that the weekday newspaper has a 52 per cent male readership.

The gender gap is more dramatic online. A Nielsen/Netratings poll in 2004 revealed that 61.8 per cent of NYTimes.com readers were men. 'In general, the number of men reading online news is eight to 13 per cent higher than women,' reported the technology magazine *Wired* ('News sites, where the men are', 4 August 2004). The article added that newspapers need not feel bad about this revelation, 'since they can demonstrate to advertisers that they have the elusive 18- to 34-year-old male – the most sought-after demographic in the media world – among their readers'. Publishers, however, wrung their hands about failing to serve 'a segment of society that's important'.

So what's causing the gender gap? The INMA's report contends that newsrooms are still male-dominated and the content of newspapers reflects this bias. In addition, newspapers target women in a ham-fisted way, trying to replicate the sort of features that appear in women's magazines – fashion, beauty, diet, relationships – but not doing it as well.

Back in 2001, former *Guardian* editor Peter Preston cast an eye over the readership gender gap and wrote: 'Background research already gives newspapers some general guidance on the differences between male and female readers. The men like news and analysis and finance and sport. The women care about news as well – their 'main reason to purchase' – but they like to be told pretty briskly what happened, not what it all may or may not mean. They are turned off by sport… and none too keen on finance, either' ('For women it's all mouth and too many trousers', *The Observer*, 9 December 2001).

Preston observed that 'women readers can be tempted in and persuaded to buy. The bad news is that the tempters and persuaders are mostly glossy mags which are expensive to produce and, worse, only work their tentative magic at weekends… ' He suggested that some newspapers had gone in 'precisely the opposite direction, pumping up sports coverage because young men allegedly like it' in a bid to boost circulation, while shelving the idea of attracting more women readers.

Few would argue with the idea that men like the sports pages. A poll conducted by *The Times* among its readers suggested that 42 per cent of men considered football coverage 'an extremely/very important' factor in their choice of daily paper, as opposed to just 7 per cent of women. As far as 'other sports' were concerned, 51 per cent of men expected their newspaper to provide extensive coverage, while only 10 per cent of women did so. Women, on the other hand, were more interested in travel, health, food and drink. (Beauty and fashion coverage were seen as less essential, reinforcing the theory that women consider these matters to be effectively addressed elsewhere.)

The Newspaper Marketing Agency in the UK has conducted research into the way men interact with the sports pages – and their responses to advertising around coverage (Men and the Sports Pages, 2005). Crucially, the men interviewed by the NMA stressed that sport was integral to their identity, 'part of being male… your father was into it too, something that was drummed into you as a kid'. The NMA confirmed the long-held theory that men turn to the sports pages first when they pick up a paper:

'Even among readers of the "qualities", more than half of men either read the back page first or just scan the front page headlines before making a beeline for the sport.'

Men use the sports pages as social oil, gathering inside information that they will use around the water cooler, the coffee machine, or at the bar after work. The sports pages are deeply entangled with male bonding rituals. 'Sport brings men together in a way nothing else can,' observes the report. 'Put a group of men of different ages, occupations, social classes, politics and cultures into a room, and it's odds-on that they'll soon be talking about sport.' The men concerned may have a wide variety of other enthusiasms, but sport is neutral territory. When it comes to their choice of newspaper, though, their decision naturally reflects their wider values, politics and social identities. That's why, argues the NMA, newspaper sports sections are ideal for targeting certain demographic groups, and thus building brands.

So what kind of advertising works best in the sports pages? The NMA says, 'Advertising that understands how high emotions run in the sports sector is particularly effective. Typically, the reader is in an intense frame of mind – mourning defeat, celebrating triumph, dreaming of future victories... He is willing to enjoy and appreciate advertising that shares this mood... '

A little obvious, perhaps – but it's certain that fans don't appreciate advertising that has been plonked down in the sports section for no apparent reason. Marketers would be unwise to underestimate the marketing savvy of sports enthusiasts. '[They] know when a brand has invested in sport,' warns the NMA. 'As one respondent said of Gillette: "They're more entitled to mention their products in relation to sport because they give money to sport."'

If you're not a sponsor, establishing relevance is all-important. This doesn't mean the brand has to be a sporting one: fans appreci- ated an ad featuring two rugby players facing off over a pint of

Guinness. The image was suitably 'mean and moody', they said, as well as providing the right 'sense of occasion'.

Another approach that works is wit. Sports fans enjoy ads that exploit major events in a smart or amusing manner. When the Greek national soccer team won the Euro 2004 tournament against all the odds, Adidas placed a full-page print ad next to the coverage. The image simply showed the celebrating team below the standard Adidas slogan, 'Impossible is nothing'. This kind of tricky, smile-provoking advertising generates a buzz around the coffee machine.

Finally, the NMA offers a word of caution. It claims that the collective identity of the sports fan is 'profoundly male' – macho, aggressive, and heroic. Any imagery that enters the scrum needs to look as though it belongs there.

NOT TAKING IT LITERALLY

Amid all this talk of magazines and newspapers, there is a serious issue that still needs to be addressed. It seems that men don't read enough novels. Men account for only 20 per cent of the fiction market, according to surveys conducted in the US, Canada and the UK ('Why women read more than men', www. npr.org, 15 September 2007). A poll released in August 2007 by the Associated Press and market researcher IPSOS found that the typical woman reads nine books in a year, compared with only five for men. Women read more than men in all categories except for history and biography.

No less an authority than the novelist Ian McEwan supports the view that women keep literature alive. In an article for *The Guardian*, he describes the experience of trying to give away free books in a central London park. The women accept them gratefully, while the men shy away ('Hello, would you like a free book?', 20

September 2005). McEwan uses this experience to demonstrate a theory that the novel was, in fact, created for women. 'A new class of leisured women not only made possible the development of this emerging literary form, but in some important degree shaped its content. The triumphant first flowering of the 18th-century novel was Richardson's *Clarissa*. Perhaps there had never been such a thorough examination of the minutiae of shifting emotions.'

It is this very emotional complexity that turns brisk, practical blokes off the novel, theorizes McEwan. '[W]omen work with a finer mesh of emotional understanding than men. The novel – by that view the most feminine of forms – answers to their biologically ordained skills... Reading groups, readings, breakdowns of book sales all tell the same story: when women stop reading, the novel will be dead.'

It is a dramatic statement, worthy of a great novelist. Men's wariness of literature may stem from childhood, when they are encouraged to be active and sporty rather than sedentary and bookish. But even keen male readers have very different preferences to women. The general consensus is that they prefer fast-paced yarns that do not get submerged in emotional entanglements.

In 2005, Professor Lisa Jardine and Anne Watkins of the University of London released the results of a study in which they interviewed men and women about books that had changed their lives. The results were startlingly different. Men were affected by books about loneliness and alienation, while women preferred to read about emotional conflict and passion. The number one book for men was *The Outsider*, by Albert Camus, followed by Joseph Conrad's *Heart of Darkness* and Dostoevsky's *Crime and Punishment*. A great many men admitted they were more affected by non-fiction, particularly history. Women most frequently cited works by Charlotte and Emily Brontë, Margaret Atwood, George Eliot and Jane Austen. They considered books to be companions and guides, and often turned back to their favourite novels for reassurance. '[Men] read novels a bit like they read photography manuals,' commented Professor Jardine, rather dismissively ('A tale of two genders: men choose novels of alienation, while women go for passion', *The Guardian*, 6 April 2006).

Men tend not to read books written by women. When bookstore chain Waterstone's asked its 5,000 staff to name their top five books, the list was dominated by male authors. A spokesman for the store said: 'Women read more than men – the core customer is a woman aged between 35 and 55 – but what they read is right across the board: chick lit, crime fiction, biographies, heavyweight novels, and they don't care about the gender of the author. Subconsciously, I think men stick to male writers. They think that what women write doesn't appeal to them.'

Book marketer Claire Round of the publisher CHA (Century Heinemann Arrow), part of Random House, says, 'You package a book differently for men than for women. For instance, women tend to be more interested in character than plot, so the book jacket reflects that. Men like action – the books of ex-SAS hero Chris Ryan, for example.'

One of the most successfully marketed books of all time is undoubtedly *The Da Vinci Code*, whose fast pace and controversial plot device – what if Jesus had a child? – crossed the gender divide. When it launched the novel in 2003, publisher Doubleday in the United States planned to build buzz even before the book came out. So it distributed 10,000 advance copies to booksellers and reviewers. To back this up, personable author Dan Brown went on a pre-publication tour of bookstores. Meanwhile, Doubleday sent constant updates about the book to an e-mail list of 300 publishing industry insiders called 'The *Da Vinci Code* noisemakers'. Outside the trade, customers were targeted with advertising posters featuring the Mona Lisa and the slogan: 'Why is this man smiling?' And when media controversy over the book's subject kicked in, it became a PR triumph. The result was six million copies in under a year.

The secret to writing a record-breaking bestseller, then, is simply to identify a theme that appeals to both sexes – and have a big marketing budget.

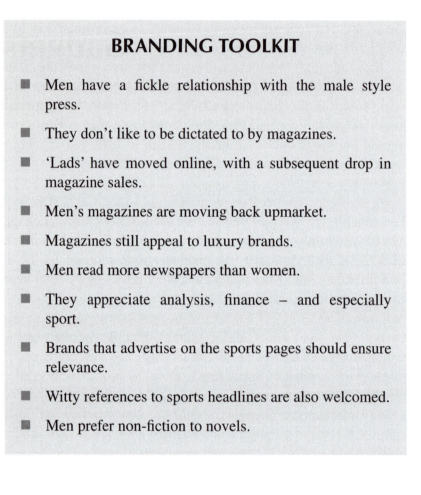

BRANDING TOOLKIT

- Men have a fickle relationship with the male style press.

- They don't like to be dictated to by magazines.

- 'Lads' have moved online, with a subsequent drop in magazine sales.

- Men's magazines are moving back upmarket.

- Magazines still appeal to luxury brands.

- Men read more newspapers than women.

- They appreciate analysis, finance – and especially sport.

- Brands that advertise on the sports pages should ensure relevance.

- Witty references to sports headlines are also welcomed.

- Men prefer non-fiction to novels.

8

Gadgets

Scene Eight: Eurostar interior, France

His BlackBerry vibrates on the tray table almost as soon as the train has swished out of the tunnel. The message is a confirmation of his meeting: 5pm at the Hotel Costes, not far from the Louvre. Provided he doesn't have to wait too long for a cab, he should have plenty of time to dump his bag at the Hilton Arc de Triomphe beforehand. Although he gets a mild kick out of staying at the Paris Hilton, it's mainly because he has the chain's loyalty card, which also gives him air miles.

He acknowledges the message with a quick thumb-tapped email. Like everyone these days, he is addicted to his BlackBerry. This version has a full keyboard as well as music, video and photo multimedia features. He admires the Apple iPhone, but he's still wary of going down that route: he gets the impression that it's not really aimed at business users, while the BlackBerry conforms to his self-image.

He doesn't think of himself as a geek – for instance, he's never been into video games – but he admits that technology and the web play a large role in his life. He can't imagine what it would be like to go back to a world without the internet. He subscribes to several email newsletters and is constantly dipping into the web for gossip about marketing, design, business and straightforward news. He has a profile on various social networking sites for self-publicity purposes. Aside from all the work-related technology, he has a nifty digital SLR camera (an Olympus E-510) and has begun to consider himself a pretty handy photographer. He even has an iPod, although he really only uses it when he goes jogging. He's downloaded a fairly sizeable playlist onto his laptop. He's also noticed that he goes to the cinema much less these days, thanks to his wide-screen TV.

TECHNOPHILIA

When Apple Inc launched the iPhone on 29 June 2007, many young men were desperate to get their hands on one. Media coverage showed male purchasers brandishing the precious package, arms flung in the air as if they'd just won a sporting event. The images revealed the competitive nature of the male hardware habit. Although women are important consumers of technology – as we'll see in a moment – men tend to be the earliest adopters of new gadgets.

The website of technology magazine *Wired* featured a few of them shortly after the iPhone came out. The most enlightening quote came from a 33-year-old online marketing consultant, who confirmed that he regularly 'splurged' on gadgets. 'It's the equivalent of having that season's handbag', he said. He admitted that he went through cell phones like some people do shoes. 'And, even though he didn't want one at first, he felt compelled to buy the Nintendo Wii game... after hearing how scarce they were... He bought the BlackBerry Pearl... only months before the iPhone was unveiled' ('Many iPhone owners relish being first', AP – Wired.com, 7 September 2007).

The same article quoted Nick Sheth, director of sales and development at retail search engine Like.com, who described technology addiction as 'a mix of vanity and function'. 'Sometimes you buy things like the iPhone that don't live up to their promise but are worth a couple of really good cocktail party conversations. Mind you, really good cocktail party conversations are very important in life.'

It seems more men than women suffer from 'gadget lust', a term employed by technology writer Adrian Kingsley-Hughes on the website ZDNet.com. According to Kingsley-Hughes, the iPod is the perfect example of a product that induces slavering desire. He observes that although it's by no means better than its competitors – in fact, it probably provides less value for money – a combination of streamlined looks and slick marketing makes it a 'must have' object. 'Both men and women are susceptible to gadget lust, although it seems that men have a much lower immunity. The theory is that this goes back to the spear and the desire to create a better, more effective pointy stick; but I think that cultural conditioning and the fact that both tech companies and marketing companies are dominated by men has a lot to do with it.' ('Do you suffer from gadget lust?', 23 October 2006.)

Men's attraction to technology may derive from their appreciation of all things functional, but there's more to it than that. Marketing experts like Apple's Steve Jobs know that form is equally important. Just as they do when they are choosing a watch or a pair of cufflinks, men look for objects that say something about themselves. Gadgets are an expression of status, as well as a means of showing that they are in tune with their times. A gadget may have a purpose, but it plays the underlying role of fashion accessory.

Psychologist Joan Harvey, of Newcastle University, told BBC. co.uk, 'Designers of technology talk about elegance, but it's really another way of saying beauty.' In other words, she believes that gadgets are jewellery for men ('Pushing your buttons', 6 July 2007). Publishers cater to gadget lust through magazines like *Stuff* and *Boys' Toys* – essentially lads' magazines fused with shopping catalogues. The latter title is an oft-used but highly appropriate term: after the childhood experience of being dragged away from toy stores, there's a subtle form of revenge in being able to run amok in an electrical department with your gold credit card.

That's if you choose to satisfy your technology urge at a store, of course. With their systematic approach to shopping – research, locate, acquire – men are ideally configured to online retail. And unlike a suit, a new PC doesn't have to be tried on before you can make a decision to buy. The web is crowded with technology sites like Uncrate, Gadgetopia, Gizmodo and Gadgetstorm.

Apple was undoubtedly the first company to realize that a computer could also be a thing of beauty – but the presence of computer technology in the home has made attractive design imperative. At the time of writing, Hewlett-Packard had launched a new range of personal computers with 'a glossy "piano black" finish, brushed aluminium mouldings and blue ambient lighting for buttons and display panels'. Head of marketing Satjiv Chahill said, 'We wanted to go for an enduring elegance in our design' ('Fashioning an image revolution for humble PCs', *Financial Times*, 12 September 2007).

But there is another good reason to make technology more aesthetically pleasing – female consumers. Recent research shows that women now buy almost as many gadgets as guys. In August 2006, the cable TV station Oxygen – 'owned and operated by women' – released a study called *Girls Gone Wired*. This revealed that women in the United States owned an average of 6.6 technology devices, as opposed to 6.9 for men. Women spend 15 hours a day 'interfacing with tech', compared to 17 hours for men. No less than 77 per cent of the women surveyed said they would prefer a new plasma TV to a diamond solitaire necklace. And 78 per cent would rather have 'a new top-of-the-line cell phone with all the latest features and a sleek design' than designer shoes.

Picking up on the research, analysts suggested that digital hardware makers had 'slept through the alarm' when it came to marketing to women. Shifting demographics meant that women now headed more households. And although they still earned less than men, their income had risen considerably since the 1970s: 'In the past three decades, men's median income has barely budged, up just 0.6 per cent, while women's has soared 63 per cent', said *Business Week*. 'Blame the male geek culture at digital hardware marketers for ignoring women in the past. As recently as 2003, Samsung Electronics tested its phones, TVs, and home theatres with all-male focus groups. Today, the company makes sure half its reviewers are women' ('Meet Jane Geek', 28 November 2005).

But if women are equally enthusiastic purchasers, attitudinal differences persist. User-friendliness is paramount for women, while multi-functionality delights many men. 'Women are busier than men', one female executive explained to *The New York Times*. 'I don't love technology enough to sit down and spend two hours with a manual like it's some great puzzle. Men get great satisfaction out of that. I'd rather read a book' ('To appeal to women, too, gadgets go beyond cute and pink', 7 June 2007).

TECHNOLOGY FOR ALL

As gadgets are now an inescapable part of all of our lives, is a purely gender-based approach to marketing becoming inappropriate? Marco Bevolo and Andreas Fruchtl, who head the foresight and trends department at Philips Design, certainly think so. Speaking for both of them, Bevolo explains, 'Due to our specific approach to research, which places more focus on societal change and cultural dynamics, we believe that it is impossible to generalize based on gender. You could actually say that gender is blurring, if not fading, and male and female attributes are becoming part of a portfolio of possible lifestyle choices.'

Bevolo points out that in some European countries, women represent the majority of high-tech students on university campuses.

'And let's not forget the steady increase of individuals living alone: in Sweden this is already more than 50 per cent of the population. In the context of the home, technology has taken over a number of traditionally burdensome "female" tasks: dishwashing, cooking, cleaning. Here high-tech plays a role in the equalization of genders.'

Although he concedes that some men use technology to demonstrate their 'manhood', he observes that the company's consumer electronic division is moving away from an angular, masculine design language – cool, metallic straight lines – towards a more feminine aesthetic: soft, calm and receiving.

Regional attitudinal differences also play a role. In Europe, Philips researchers found that high-tech devices were required to fit in to an existing lifestyle, expressing cultural values or a general vision of life. In the United States, technology is used to demonstrate social status. In China, it's an ostentatious expression of coolness, modernity and success. 'What is crucial is to know what people want to get out of their high-tech artefacts and then design accordingly,' Bevolo says.

Philips' design is targeted at individual needs rather than genders. The research carried out by the company is rich and deep – from ethnographic studies in the home to predictions of future cultural change. In order to bring findings alive for designers, it develops 'personas', fictional characters that capture the essence of research findings with the immediacy of a biography, a narrative slice of somebody's life. 'Instead of categorizing people's preferences as "male" or "female" we would address socio-cultural and lifestyle preferences as "Betty's" or "Ronald's" or "Hiroshi's". For each person, a rich set of preferences, needs and demands.'

One thing we can be certain of is that technology will soon merge seamlessly with our homes. 'The home of the future will look much more like the home of the past than the home of today. Technology will be naturally dematerialized and diffused, with no need of wires and black boxes. The inevitable ability of high-tech to become more human and flexible will offer endless opportunities to design around people's emotional and cultural preferences.'

Even the most 'masculine' of objects already incorporate a synthesis of 'male' and 'female' design attributes, Bevolo and Fruchtl say. 'As a strong example, it is known through our consumer research that electric shavers are mostly purchased by women as gifts for their male partners. Here, the design and communication strategies must clearly incorporate these female decision makers, despite the fact that the actual product will be used by males.'

THE GAMES MEN PLAY

When brands wish to target young men, advertising within video games is an increasingly popular strategy. While the movie industry struggles with online piracy and broadcasters deal with competition from the internet, the gaming industry is growing. It was said to be worth more than US$20 billion at the time of writing, and PricewaterhouseCoopers predicts that the figure will rise to US$54.6 billion within a couple of years. There are around 132 million gamers in the US alone. And they are not, if they ever were, just spotty teens barricaded in their bedrooms: research by the media analyst Initiative Futures and Technologies in New York has shown that even hardcore gamers tend to be aged between 18 and 34. Big brands that regularly advertise within games include Sony Ericsson, Nike and Coca-Cola.

Until recently, the most typical form of in-game advertising, as with the FIFA soccer game, involved placing logos on perimeter hoardings and score boards. But approaches are becoming more sophisticated. For Test Drive Unlimited, a multiplayer videogame from Atari, men's fashion retailer Ben Sherman enabled gamers to buy clothes in a 3-D replica of one of its real-world stores. The clothing brand Diesel has dressed characters in a number of videogames. Some brands are even contributing entire sub-plots. Visa recently introduced its anti-fraud technology into a game based on the hugely successful crime series *CSI*.

Other advertisers prefer to create branded games within their own websites, a strategy known as 'advergaming'. Initiative has created games for clients like Vauxhall and easyGroup, the company behind UK-based budget airline easyJet. In Austria, the agency developed an 'advergame' aimed at young men for the Axe brand.

But while advergaming puts clients in the driving seat, it's more challenging to insert your brand into a game conceived by a third party. The problem with console games is that advertisers can't change their ad once the product is on shelves. With an online game, they can go back and reconsider their strategy.

There's also a debate about how much advertising gamers can take in. Sophisticated eye-tracking tests suggest consumers are so busy concentrating on the game that ads escape their attention. Nonetheless, brands will continue to search for ways of monitoring and improving the effectiveness of in-game advertising. A clear indication of this came in April 2006, when Microsoft paid a reported US$400 million for a company called Massive Incorporated, which specializes in placing ads in games. Yankee Group, a Boston-based research firm, predicts that advertisers will spend US$730 million on in-game advertising and product placement by 2010. Soon, even the most conservative brands will realize that this is one game they can't afford not to play.

BRANDING TOOLKIT

- For men, the latest tech item is 'the equivalent of this season's handbag'.

- A new gadget is a conversation piece, 'a mixture of vanity and function'.

- Women are also enthusiastic technology purchasers.

- They appreciate ease of use, while men enjoy multi-functionality.

- But gender approaches to technology are blurring – an important trend.

- Advertising in gaming is still an under-exploited means of reaching men.

9

Hotels

Scene Nine: Taxicab interior, Paris, France

He gazes out of the taxi window with a faint smile of satisfaction on his face. The radio is playing Senegalese music at full blast and the driver is complaining about something – or everything – in a torrent of French that's too rapid to comprehend. But he doesn't care: the meeting went well and the hardest part of the day is over.

As he had predicted, he'd been able to check into his room at the Hilton before making the short hop across town to the Hotel Costes. The Costes was a rather pretentious place tricked out in mock 17th century style – heavy on the gilt and the plush velvet – and patronized by models and rock stars. It was part of a mini-empire of Paris hotels and restaurants run by the enigmatic Costes brothers, Jean-Louis and Gilbert. But the music in its bar was so good that its DJ had released a compilation album – and then another, and another – and now the Costes name was known to urban nomads all over the world. He'd not been surprised that the owners of a fashion brand had chosen to meet him there.

The meeting took place, not in the bar, but at a little table in the Italianate courtyard, over tea. His potential clients were a heavily built man with a saturnine, Mediterranean complexion, and the company's head of marketing, a stylish woman called Sandrine. His tone was light yet professional as he took them through the credentials presentation and offered a brief analysis of their current strategy. At one point he'd leaned forward to sketch an idea for their new logo on a paper napkin – he'd sensed they'd liked that. When they shook hands at the end of the meeting, there seemed little doubt that the agency was in the running for the job. He also thought that Sandrine eyed his business card speculatively, but he couldn't be sure.

Now he's heading back to the Hilton to give Bernard the good news and check his e-mails before planning his evening in Paris. He's glad he managed to justify an overnight stay by promising to catch up with one of the agency's contacts – a freelance graphic designer – the next morning. These days he thinks of hotel rooms as decompression chambers; escape pods where he can unwind in a neutral space for a few hours.

ROOMS WITH ALL THE TRIMMINGS

Hotel chains love business travellers. For a start, business people often stay during the week, meaning that they can be charged steeper rates than weekend visitors. Through various incentives they can be converted into loyal clients, returning to stay at branches of the same hotel chain around the world and encouraging their colleagues to do so. What's more, they are likely to rack up bigger bills, being unafraid to dive into the mini-bar or entertain business contacts in the hotel restaurant.

And those are not their only indulgences. In 2005, a survey by the British hotel brand Travelodge discovered that workers in the UK spent more than £1.3 billion a year on business travel. Based on a survey of more than 700 companies, the research revealed that employees took around 14 million overnight business trips a year. Nearly half the companies did not put an automatic cap on business trip expenses, while two in five employees were allowed to make their own travel and accommodation arrangements. No less than 38 per cent stayed in four- or five-star hotels while travelling on business.

Reports of self-indulgent behaviour while travelling for work are legion. Another survey, this time by the website Tripadvisor.com, revealed that 12 per cent of the respondents had visited a strip club during a business trip. Luxury sheets and free bath products were listed among their favourite perks. Not only that, but 'pornographic movies account for 60–80 per cent of the average hotel's in-room entertainment revenues – a lucrative haul given that the average duration of a viewing is less than five minutes' ('What men really get up to on business trips', *The Times*, 30 October 2006).

And while independent leisure travellers often seek quirky, one-off 'boutique' hotels, business people have no problem with chains. In fact, they often feel comfortable in the knowledge that a certain brand of hotel is going to vary only infinitesimally depending on its location. That's why hotel brands work so hard to attract business travellers – and keep them. Like advertising agencies opening overseas outposts, they follow their customers around the world in hot pursuit of the global economy. Right now they are busily building a presence in mainland China.

Apart from a well-stocked mini bar and a full line-up of pay-per-view movies, what do businessmen look for in a hotel? Mike Ashton, senior vice-president, marketing of Hilton Hotels, says the tools that allow them to work efficiently – seamless internet access, fax machines and so forth – are now mandatory. 'Beyond that, it's about shaping an experience that allows the business person to feel more effective than they would at another hotel. And the competition is intense – we compete directly with brands such as Marriot, Sheraton and Intercontinental, and indirectly with lifestyle brands, mid-market brands and luxury hotels.' If people choose Hilton, says Ashton, it's because they have confidence in the brand. 'It's a very emotional choice.'

Around the world, hotels are tempting business travellers in increasingly extravagant ways. 'Pillow menus' are by no means uncommon. You're allergic to feathers? No problem: pick your preferred filling, size and plumpness from a wide range. Talking of menus, the room service meal offering is crucial – business travellers demand plenty of healthy options, available 24/7. Health clubs and pools are also becoming obligatory. Toronto-based luxury hotel group Fairmont Hotels and Resorts discovered that 70 per cent of its guests use its gyms twice a week. So it allowed members of its President's Club loyalty scheme to reserve Adidas apparel and footwear in their sizes and have the gym kit waiting for them in their rooms when they arrived. Businessmen like nothing better than to travel light – and this initiative means they no longer have to pack their gym shoes. Some hotels will even include an iPod loaded with their favourite exercising songs.

With brands struggling to outdo one another, the human touch can make a difference. The concierge has taken on a renewed importance, evolving into a combination of city insider, counsellor and fixer. Need tickets for that sold-out show? We'll see what we can do. Have to organise a reception for 15 clients? Leave it to us. There are reports of hotels hiring the former personal assistants of demanding bosses – movie studio executives, rock stars and other celebrities – on exorbitant salaries to smooth the stays of their guests. Elsewhere, hotels are upgrading their corporate entertainment facilities. The Kempinski Atlantic in Hamburg has a luxurious private cinema for up to eight people that can be hired for €150 (or €450 for the whole day).

But Hilton's Mike Ashton says the real difference is made in more subtle ways. 'The service must be absolutely consistent from country to country. That provides a very high comfort factor. The in-room experience is vital because business people value their "me time" – a few hours when they can finally relax. And it goes without saying that they should feel totally at ease throughout their stay – their arrival and departure should be smooth.'

Luxury brand Peninsula Hotels – which has eight properties, three in the United States and five in Asia – can send a chauffeur-driven Rolls-Royce to pick up certain of its guests, if required. The hotels are known for their sumptuous restaurants and well-appointed fitness centres, which provide personal trainers. 'Men increasingly require spa facilities and massage,' says Jean Forrest, the group's general manager of marketing. 'Business people have such frantic lifestyles that they take any opportunity they can to relax. It helps them work more efficiently afterwards.'

The Peninsula is proud of the technological aspects of its rooms – satellite radio and TV, an iPod dock – including the bedside master panel that controls light and heat. There's also a 'butler button' with which guests can summon the valet, who can take a suit and return it pressed within one hour.

Customization is becoming a useful point of differentiation. Thanks to forms completed in rooms or on their websites, many hotels now keep a record of their guests' preferences so they can cater to them during their next stay. This can range from the hypoallergenic pillow option to the contents of the mini bar or even the exact temperature of the room when they arrive.

Mike Ashton confirms: 'All our research shows that business customers want to feel as if they are being treated differently, a little better. That's particularly important for members of our loyalty programme. These customers require a sense of exclusivity, as if everything is being done to allow them to work more efficiently. They want to feel recognized.'

Hilton's loyalty scheme is the typographically awkward Hilton Hhonors, which provides points with every stay and allows guests to redeem them at any of the group's properties around the world. Many people, of course, collect points while on business and then redeem them at resort hotels when they take vacations with their families. The Hilton scheme is attractive because it provides both loyalty points and air miles.

Hotels tend to market themselves through the business press – the Peninsula cites the *Financial Times*, the *International Herald Tribune* and *Forbes* as typical advertising vehicles – but they also want to establish a personal relationship with their customers. This can be done via conventional direct marketing or email newsletters – which offer those who sign up preferential rates or package deals on leisure-oriented weekend breaks. The Peninsula's Jean Forrest adds, 'Many large corporations have their own on-site travel manager, so we try to form relationships with them in the hope that we will become one of the company's preferred hotel brands.'

The Hotel Costes in Paris is a much more bijou affair than the stately edifices of the Peninsula chain – but it has a brand profile far out of proportion to its modest size. As we've already heard, the hotel was created by Paris restaurateurs Jean-Louis and Gilbert Costes. Like many of those in the Paris restaurant trade, the brothers hail from the Auvergne region of France, where their mother Marie-Josèphe had turned the family farm into a successful inn. When they came to Paris, they could have easily ended up like so many Auvergnats before them – waiting tables in noisy *brasseries* or running bistros. Instead, in 1983, they bought a modest café in Les Halles and turned it into the hippest destination in the city, thanks to cutting edge design by Philippe Starck. Today they own some of the best-located restaurants in Paris, from the elegant glass menagerie atop the Pompidou Centre – Le Georges – to the restaurant overlooking the pyramid at the Louvre – Café Marly – and the terrace where the fashion set go to preen and be seen – L'Avenue, in Avenue Montaigne.

They acquired the location that became the Hotel Costes from the Hilton group for a reported US$25 million in the early 1990s, re-opening it in 1995. This time the interior was by Jacques Garcia, who channelled his enthusiasm for the 17th and early 18th centuries to create a baroque fantasyland – a softly-lit labyrinth of mirrors, ferns and gilt. Guests had the delicious sensation that they were entering a restored bordello. The decadence struck a chord with the newly rich. At the same time, the hotel courted the TV channel Canal Plus, ensuring that many of the international guests who appeared on the broadcaster's late night chat show ended up staying at the Costes. Dustin Hoffman is said to be a regular guest. Johnny Depp and Vanessa Paradis supposedly met there. Sharon Stone and Madonna have also been spotted several times, according to the French press ('*Les dessous d'un empire*', *L'Express*, 11 May 2006).

The celebrity factor was boosted by the hotel's in-house DJ, Stéphane Pompougnac. He joined the hotel in 1997 and his mixes – a silky blend of house, lounge and laidback pop – became so popular with guests that he was encouraged to release a compilation album, which appeared in 1999. The bestselling disc and its sequels (nine of them at the time of writing) have made the Costes a byword for Parisian chic around the world. Logically, the hotel has followed this up with branded toiletries, scented candles and room perfume.

As with any other brand, hotels have certain values and attributes that their guests appreciate. The Costes is all about networking and flirting in a seductive environment. The Peninsula plays on the mythology surrounding its original Hong Kong hotel, established in the 1920s as the 'Grande Dame of the Far East'. As well as its fleet of Rolls-Royce Silver Phantoms, it boasts a helipad on the roof. Afternoon tea in the lobby is a Hong Kong institution. Ironically, though, it's not a business hotel. 'Few business people who come to Hong Kong want to stay on the Kowloon side, unless they have meetings there,' admits Jean Forrest, 'but the hotel's heritage and iconic status form the roots of our brand. Our hotels in the United States are more business-oriented – and the Peninsula in Manila has something like 80 per cent business occupancy.'

Hilton, on the other hand, has a slightly mixed identity. Ashton says, 'In the fifties and sixties, Hilton Hotels had an extremely prestigious, sexy and cool image, which they retain in some cities.

The hotels have a certain international cachet, and you'll see stars getting their photographs taken outside. Elsewhere the brand has a more reliable, understated feel about it.'

So what about Paris Hilton, the ultimate heiress? Although the high-profile socialite is not linked to the group in a business sense (her grandfather, Barron Hilton, was the son of Hilton Hotels founder Conrad Hilton), surely her name and media presence affect the brand? 'I don't think it does any harm at all,' says Ashton, good-humouredly. 'It means the Hilton name is constantly in the press. And if you look at our customer profile, it tends to be the older, male business traveller. Media coverage of Paris Hilton tends to attract the attention of a younger audience, so in that respect it's great for us.'

BAD BEHAVIOUR IS GOOD FOR BUSINESS

A hint of naughtiness is not necessarily a bad thing for a travel destination. To a certain extent we travel to escape ourselves – or at least, our humdrum quotidian existence. Businessmen are not immune to this urge. As we've seen, they consume adult entertainment via their in-room pay TV services. Single male travellers are also good news for escort services and lap dancing clubs. Of course, many of them pursue innocent activities that they don't get a chance to indulge in when hampered by work or family responsibilities: a visit to a museum or a whiz around a golf course; a gourmet meal followed by a couple of whiskies at a jazz club. Magazines regularly run '24 hours in…' articles catering to business travellers who find time for a little pleasure.

The allure of the faintly illicit was taken to its logical conclusion by the city of Las Vegas in 2003. Following the 2001 terrorist attacks and a relaxation of gambling regulations elsewhere in the United States, the number of tourists visiting the city had slumped from 35.8 million in 2000 to 35 million two years later (Encyclopaedia of Major Marketing Campaigns, Volume 2, 2007). Realizing it had to do something to stop the drain, the Las Vegas Convention & Visitors Authority decided to rebrand Vegas as a broad leisure destination, shifting the focus away from gambling.

The US$58 million advertising campaign, created by local agency R&R Partners, was launched in January 2003 across every medium: TV, print, outdoor and internet. Using the slogan 'What happens here, stays here', the ads featured people who had recently returned from trips to Vegas. When they were asked what they'd gotten up to there, they became shifty and embarrassed. Some made up transparently flimsy stories. The first television spots portrayed Las Vegas as a place where normally upright people lived double lives, engaged in one night stands or indulged in heavy drinking. But the transgressions were okay because they happened in Vegas, where normal rules didn't apply.

At first, somewhat hypocritically, local businesses were irritated by the suggestion that the city of Las Vegas encouraged immoral – or at the very least irresponsible – behaviour. To add to the controversy, the ads were banned from the 2003 Super Bowl broadcast. But marketing experts loved the campaign, showering it with awards. So, apparently, did the public: by 2004, the visitor numbers were almost back up to 38 million again. Copywriter Jeff Candido explained to the *Washington Post*, '[The ads are] successful because people can imagine much more than we show. A grandmother who sees these spots can imagine that [the debauchery] is spending too much time at the buffet. The 23-year-old bachelor party guys can have their own idea about what went on' ('Las Vegas ads' winning streak', 2 December 2004).

The campaign was designed to appeal to many different consumers, who had little in common except that they were adult and not averse to a bit of fun. But the slogan 'What happens here, stays here' has an undeniably masculine edge, as if plucked from a movie about mobsters. And in the minds of many male business travellers, the phrase could apply to practically any solo trip.

BRANDING TOOLKIT

■ Standard business services – such as internet access – are now obligatory.

■ Service must be absolutely seamless from arrival to departure.

■ Businessmen increasingly require a fitness centre option.

■ Spas, massages and healthy option meals also score highly.

■ Loyalty cards and bonus points systems can ensure fidelity, but members of such schemes expect 'better' treatment.

■ Customization is important: take a note of their preferences.

■ Men use 'me time' on business trips to indulge themselves.

10

Pictures

Scene Ten: Hilton Arc de Triomphe Hotel,
Paris, France

He's stayed at the hotel so often that it's beginning to feel like a home away from home. In his room, he kicks off his shoes, loosens his tie and sprawls luxuriously on the bed. He's made his calls and checked his mails – now he's cruising towards evening. The TV remote is in his hand. Leaning on an elbow, he flicks through the channels, waiting for something to catch his eye. He pauses briefly at CNN, but soon moves on to Eurosport. A rugby game is in progress. This seems to fit his surroundings – the French are almost as keen on rugby as the English. He finds televized sport comforting: there's something timeless about the muddy green field and the swift familiar movements of the players. He can take in the images while his mind ticks over.

A free night looms ahead. Maybe he'll catch a movie at one of the many cinemas along the Champs-Elysées – most of them show American films in their original language, with French subtitles. After that, he knows a quiet bistro called the Tir Bouchon, where he can take a table at the back and read his mystery novel, drinking a couple of glasses of good red wine.

He's beginning to look forward to this when the phone rings, startling him. It's Sandrine, the woman from the meeting. 'We're very pleased with the way things went today,' she tells him. 'If you haven't got any plans, we'd be delighted to invite you to dinner.'

The 'we' hangs there suggestively – dinner with Sandrine *and* her boss. But it's still a better option than dining alone. He accepts politely. *'Très bien,'* she says. 'The restaurant is called L'Alcazar, in Saint Germain. Rue Mazarine. We'll be dining rather late, I'm afraid, at around nine.'

He tells her that will be fine – he still has a little work to do. Then he hangs up and returns to the rugby match.

THE POWER OF TV SPORT

Watching sport on television is one of the most popular male pastimes. It is also one of the most federating. In a world where TV viewing is increasingly 'time-shifted' – recorded for later consumption – live sports events are almost the only broadcasts that still have the power to bring people together around a television screen at an appointed hour. So far, the internet and mobile technology have had little impact on the TV audiences of live sporting occasions. It's no wonder, then, that advertisers can't get enough sports.

The post-war arrival of TV had a seismic effect on the structure and financing of sport. Until that time, of course, the organizers of sporting events had relied largely on ticket sales to finance stadiums and the salaries of professional players. But just as television companies discovered that the pace and drama of sports broadcasts had a magnetic appeal for viewers – and therefore advertisers – the sports sector quickly realized that advertising and sponsorship represented major new sources of revenue. Although ticket sales remained important – particularly to organisers of corporate entertainment – brands were now the ultimate backers. 'Suddenly, sport became not just business, but big business... In some eyes, sport itself mutated into a means to an end, a component of an entertainment package – important, but only part of a total entertainment offering capable of bringing in fans and generating revenue' (Encyclopaedia of Global Industries, Gale, 2006: World Advertising Research Centre).

Frenzied by the prospect of large TV audiences, the bright logos of brands alighted on sporting events like rapacious birds. As well as advertising around broadcasts and placing hoardings alongside pitches, brands made their mark on clothing, teams, leagues and individual players. And if that wasn't enough to get noticed, they built whole new stadiums. Industries that faced television and print advertising restrictions – notably alcohol and tobacco – found an ideal alternative in sports sponsorship.

Players are enormously powerful role models for young men. This hero worship starts young. As one father commented, 'When I take my kid out and hit him ground balls at shortstop, he wants to be [baseball star] Derek Jeter. He doesn't want to be me' ('Sports celebrity influence on the behavioural intentions of Generation Y', *Journal of Advertising Research*, Vol. 44, No. 1, March 2004). The choices that sports heroes make – whether in reality or in advertising campaigns – undoubtedly affects the comportment of their fans. The commercialization of sport transformed the status of players. Instead of negotiating directly with sports clubs, they now acted like highly-paid celebrities, with agents who could negotiate huge fees – as well as lucrative advertising and sponsorship deals. When Tom Cruise cried 'Show me the money!' in the film *Jerry Maguire* (1996), he was of course playing a sports agent. By 2004, 'the top 50 highest-paid athletes in the world had a combined income of US$1.1 billion, 40 per cent of which was from individual endorsements' (WARC).

That same year, the National Football League reaped US$5.3 billion in revenues, followed by US$4.3 billion for Major League Baseball, US$2.9 billion for the National Basketball Association, and US$2.2 billion for the National Hockey League. Meanwhile, the top 25 soccer teams in Europe raked in a combined total of US$4.2 billion.

Soccer, as we'll deign to call it for American readers, is the world's most popular televized sport. With its multiracial, good-looking, highly paid players – who often come from humble backgrounds – and its ability to evoke a tribal sense of belonging, 'the beautiful game' delivers a heady cocktail for spectators and advertisers. No less than 5.9 billion viewers around the globe tuned in to the 2006 World Cup, with 284 million people watching the final (according to the media buying agency Initiative). Manchester United is the most popular team *of any kind* in the world, with a global fan base of 75 million worldwide. In 2000, Nike signed a £300 million deal to provide the club's kit over a 13 year period. And in 2006, the insurer American International Group signed a four-year, £56 million deal to place its logo on the team's shirts.

Needless to say, the crowds of attentive television viewers and the advertisers that flock around them have combined with the increasing number of channels to create intense competition over sports broadcasting rights. In March 2007, for example, commercial broadcaster ITV and the Irish broadcaster Setanta made headlines in the UK when they scooped the rights to show all of the English national soccer team's home international matches, plus the FA Cup, for four years. The deal meant the Football Association pocketed £425 million. (The rights had previously been split between Sky and the BBC.)

But football – or soccer, if you prefer – is by no means the only game in town. During the run-up to the 2008 Beijing Olympics, the media buying agency Zenith-Optimedia estimated that the Games would pull in an extra US$900 million in advertising for China. It added that the Olympics would contribute a further US$3 billion to the world advertising economy ('Advertisers and sponsors going for gold at Beijing Olympics', *The Times*, 14 September 2007). And well before the echo of the first starting pistol had died away in Beijing, the organizers of the 2012 Olympics in London were hoping to reap over £2 billion in sponsorship deals, which would enable them to cover the huge cost of staging the Games and maybe turn a profit. 'Although branding seems the obvious reason to put your company's name to the Games, there are other factors such as improved government relations, boosting staff morale or simply blocking a rival,' commented *The Independent*. ('London Olympics team sets sights on sponsorship gold', 5 May 2006.) The article explained that 10 'tier one' sponsors would pay between £50 million and £100 million for the right to use the Olympic rings, 'arguably the world's most marketable symbol'.

Away from these global events, however, there's a powerful sports franchise that many Europeans have barely heard of: NASCAR. In the United States, however, the National Association of Stock Car Auto Racing is a marketing dynamo. A 2005 report revealed that '72% of racing fans report they consciously purchase NASCAR sponsors' products, and 40% say they would switch to brands that become official promoters. 57% of NASCAR followers place a higher level of trust in sponsors' brands than in their non-supporting competitors' ('An exploratory investigation into NASCAR fan culture', *Sport Marketing Quarterly*, Vol. 14, 2005).

This sense of loyalty is catnip for brands like Gillette, which signed a US$20 million a year marketing deal with NASCAR in 2003, adding to its portfolio of soccer, baseball, basketball, golf and hockey events. But it's worth disclosing here that 40 per cent of NASCAR fans are, in fact, women. The sport attracts a wide range of enthusiasts. The association says one in three US adults – or 75 million people – are NASCAR fans. It adds that 17 of the top 20 most attended sporting events in the country are NASCAR events. And it is the second-most watched sport on TV after National Football League games. As well as the obvious attractions of speed and excitement, NASCAR benefits from a position as a 'family' sport: its drivers are seen as accessible and down-to-earth. But it has played another smart trick, too.

'NASCAR has educated fans about the sport's economics. For example, a team can spend up to US$1 million a year just on tyres. As a result, 76 per cent of fans agree with the statement that without sponsors, the sport would not exist. Almost two-thirds say they don't mind paying more for a sponsor's products... Fully one-half of NASCAR fans say they consider buying sponsors' products as their contribution to the sport's well-being' ('NASCAR's marketing prowess a biz model', *Atlanta Business Chronicle*, 26 May 2006).

Far more international – and elitist – than NASCAR is Formula One motor racing. This has a symbolic masculine appeal, from the aggressive shape of the cars, to the faintly phallic form of the drivers' headgear, right down to the creamy gouts of champagne that are sprayed over pretty girls by the victor. And indeed, according to research in the UK from Mintel, motor racing appeals far more to men than to women. Quizzed about their sporting interests, 30.5 per cent of male respondents named motor racing, while it figured on the list of only 13 per cent of women. Mintel adds that Formula One and its lesser cousins, although far less physically accessible than football, are very popular on television. 'If the coverage of all the different types of sport is combined, [motor sport] is actually the second biggest behind football, with nearly 221,000 minutes of coverage in 2005' (Motor Sports, UK, February 2007).

When Martini wanted to raise its profile among young men, it funded a motor racing TV series called *The Martini World Circuit*, creating a website to back up the property. It negotiated sponsorship of the Ferrari Formula One team and established signage at races in Barcelona, Milan and Monte Carlo. *Campaign* magazine summed up: 'It's a well thought-through association between a brand that still has Côte d'Azure, Riva speedboats and Cary Grant old-world glamour and a sport that has that rare combination of testosterone and style. The glove fits' ('Martini targets young men via Ferrari', 9 March 2007). Other alcohol brands – such as Budweiser and Johnnie Walker whisky – have also sponsored motor racing. Any criticism of the link between drinking and driving is dismissed with the justification that the targets are sitting at home in front of their televisions, rather than behind the wheels of their cars.

Perhaps as a counterbalance to the roaring machismo of motor racing, the sedate pastime of golf is also valued by marketers to men. In the UK, 81 per cent of golfers are male and 86 per cent fit into the wealthy, upmarket ABC1 category, according to sports marketing company IMG. And if you thought they were all middle-aged businessmen, think again – IMG says 43.5 per cent are 25-to-44-year-olds, while an appealing 20 per cent are aged between 15 and 24. And 71 per cent of those who watch televised golf are male, too ('The right sport', *Campaign*, 4 April 2003).

Matching brand to sport can be a delicate affair. Products that have obvious links with sport and put something back into it are accepted, and even welcomed, by fans. Nike and its arch-rival Adidas have come to symbolize the relationship between brands and sport. Nike founder Phil Knight established a symbiotic relationship with the brand's advertising agency, Wieden & Kennedy, right from the start. Although he considered most advertising banal, Knight had no illusions about its power. In 1987, then Nike marketing chief Scott Bedury asked for a whopping increase in the brand's advertising budget, from US$8 million to US$34 million. 'Knight asked him the one question he hadn't prepped for: "How do we know you're asking for enough?" That year, Nike spent a jaw-dropping US$48 million' ('The new Nike', *Business Week*, 20 September 2004).

Together, Nike and its agency have produced dramatic, highly memorable campaigns – running in parallel to numerous hefty sponsorship deals – that send branded gear leaping from shelves.

But sports fans won't take any old branding. Writing in *The Advertiser* in 2004, Michael O'Hara Lynch of Visa recalled the furore that broke out when Major League Baseball announced plans to place *Spiderman II* movie logos on bases during certain games. 'It was an example of the consequences when sports and entertainment converge, and fans do not provide their approval,' he wrote. 'The involvement of marketing in sports and entertainment is done by permission of the fan. We as marketers must respect the relationship that exists, and work within the parameters of what is acceptable to the avid fan... We must... keep a laser-like focus on providing real value to the fans, because building loyalty with them is the most effective way to derive value from a sports sponsorship' ('Marketers should proceed with caution when trying to integrate sports with entertainment', August 2004).

The melding of a movie for young adults – one that had little or no connection to sports – with baseball felt all wrong to the fans. And when they expressed their outrage through the media, the campaign was pulled.

HOW MEN WATCH SPORTS

America's sports broadcasting mastodon is ESPN. Almost 30 years old, the Entertainment and Sports Programming Network is carried by almost every cable and satellite provider in the United States and is considered an essential partner by most sports franchises. Its original cable channel is available in more than 90 million homes – more than any other cable network – while its five other domestic channels have equally massive coverage. It is also a global brand, serving 194 countries in 12 languages.

Like the other media monoliths, ESPN has extended its brand, launching a magazine that now has two million subscribers, and a website that has 17 million unique visitors a month. These figures are not so much a reflection of the power of the ESPN brand as a testament to the public's hunger for sports information. And with consumers come advertisers: according to *The Washington Times*, the brand's annual revenues are around US$7 billion ('ESPN evolves with new media', 25 September 2006).

But ESPN is not infallible. Its mobile phone service, ESPN Mobile, was abandoned in late 2006 after failing to attract subscribers. Most analysts blamed the fact that customers were required to sign up with the new carrier, as well as shelling out for a US$400 ESPN-branded phone. Instead, ESPN has returned to delivering real-time scores and video clips to other cellular providers. It may simply have been too early into the market – as discussed earlier, an image on a mobile phone screen, however convenient for sneaky match-watching at work or on the move, does nothing to convey the drama of stadium sports.

In Europe, ESPN has a serious rival in the form of Eurosport – the biggest European sports satellite and cable network, owned by French broadcaster TF1. It's available in 20 different languages and reaches 110 million homes and 240 million viewers across 59 countries. Eurosport is closely in tune with the needs of its viewers and has firm views about the way they consume sport. In particular, it has conducted two major studies concerning male viewers.

Marketing director Roberto Passariello says, 'A lot of the things that might easily be dismissed as clichés are actually true. Let's take 16- to 20-year-old men, for example. They are still feeling a little lost and insecure, so sport for them is necessarily tribal – it's almost like getting a tattoo or a piercing; a badge of honour. For that reason, this group almost uniformly loves football, with its accent on the team. They're also suckers for brands, although they'll tell you that they're not.'

By their mid-twenties, men are in their first responsible jobs and find that they have much less time on their hands. Many of them still think of themselves as sportsmen, although they rarely play. 'For them, sport has become a form of social recognition. They use it to start conversations and fuel friendships. That's why they love facts and statistics. At this stage, sport is also part of the fabric of office life – which is why so many offices start softball or football teams.'

Passariello describes middle age – 45 to 55 – as 'the most difficult period' in a man's life. 'He's probably got a high-level job with lots of stress. He may be going through a divorce. His kids are growing up and the generation gap is beginning to show. He might also be questioning his masculinity – am I still attractive? This is when you might find him playing tennis or squash in order to get back in shape. For him, televised sport is an escape, a form of entertainment. It's also often a way of communicating with his kids. He may not like their music or movies, but at least he can talk to them about the football.'

Eurosport's research showed that these different life stages and attitudes varied very little across borders – European men have similar responses to sport. Passariello also questions the idea that women are becoming soccer fans. 'The viewing figures are up, but when you talk to them about football, the reasons they give for watching it paint a whole new picture. A lot of them say they watch because they want to support the men in their lives – to spend time with them and share a moment of excitement and bonding. The truth is that, left to their own devices, women are more impressed by individual achievement. For exercise, they'll run or swim – or they'll take up a spiritually cleansing activity like yoga. They're also into aesthetics. As viewers, their preferred sports are swimming, figure skating and gymnastics.'

Fear not, though – in this age of masculine experimentation, men are taking up yoga too. A Harris poll commissioned by – who else? – *Yoga Journal* in the United States showed that men made up 23 per cent of America's 15 million adepts. Writing about the study for *Newsweek*, yoga enthusiast John Capouya commented, 'They're in it for the exercise and the physical benefits – hold the chanting and the New Age vibes' ('Real men do yoga', 16 June 2003). Some used yoga to limber up for different sports, while others found that it cured back pain. The article explained that men favoured fast-moving styles such as Vin-yasa and Ashtanga, sometimes known as 'power yoga'. A useful phrase if your goal is to re-brand yoga for a male market.

PRODUCT PLACEMENT – BRANDING BOND

But the best way to sell yoga – or anything – to a man is probably to get James Bond to do it. Product placement in action movies is an ideal way of targeting males, and Bond is the ultimate action franchise.

Brands have long been aware of the advantages of working products seamlessly into existing pieces of entertainment. Chanel created costumes for Jean Renoir's film *La Règle du Jeu* in 1941; and the outfits worn by Delphine Seyrig in *L'Année Dernière à Marienbad* (1961) helped to rekindle the designer's prestige after the shaky post-war period. Hubert Givenchy benefited from a lengthy creative partnership with Audrey Hepburn, outfitting her in film after film. In a masculine context, Giorgio Armani famously negotiated a deal to dress Richard Gere in the film *American Gigolo* (1980). The effect on sales was so spectacular that Armani made product placement a central pillar of his strategy. His name has appeared in the credits of more than 300 movies. Watch an Armani-clad film like *The Untouchables* (1987) and you can't help wishing you dressed like its leading men.

With advertising avoidance growing common among TV viewers, we'll see an increasing amount of product placement on the small screen. In 2005, a Zero Halliburton attaché case became a plot device in the series *Lost*. A year later, auto maker Nissan placed no less than 10 vehicles in the first season of sci-fi drama *Heroes*, and used the second season to promote its Rogue auto. Similarly, the action hero Jack Bauer (Kiefer Sutherland) – in many ways a distant relative of Bond – drives a Ford Expedition and wears an MTM Special Ops watch in the series *24*. These deals fuel endless debates on the internet, which only enhances their effectiveness.

On the big screen, though, Bond is the ultimate branded male – and he's been at it right from the start. Author Ian Fleming scattered brands throughout the Bond books to add authenticity to his outlandish plots and create a luxurious universe for his hero. He knew that the function of the novels was escapist – readers would aspire to being Bond, or at least somebody who moved in his circles. Much like Bond himself – who is a far more human figure in the books than he became in the films – the objects described are not whimsical gadgets, but tantalisingly real products. Any fan of the books is familiar with Bond's Rolex Oyster Perpetual Chronometer, his Sea Island cotton shirts, his battered pigskin Revelation suitcase and his Ronson lighter. The literary Bond drives a Bentley – the Aston Martin only crops up in the novel *Goldfinger* – and washes his hair with Pinaud Elixir, 'that prince among shampoos' (*On Her Majesty's Secret Service*). And as Bond has a sharp eye for the products used by others, the full list of brands cited in the books is far longer. In his exhaustive and frequently hilarious (2006) book *The Man Who Saved Britain*, Simon Winder writes: '*Moonraker* becomes the Book of Genesis for the brand-name consumerism that dominates our world, with each chapter constituting a wilderness of eating, drinking and behavioural tips'.

With so much branding going on in the source material, it was inevitable that the films should become popular product placement vehicles. This begins early in the series. As in the books, the Aston Martin makes its debut in *Goldfinger*. But Bond drives various models throughout the movies, infrequently replaced by Lotuses or BMWs if somebody comes up with a better offer. The payoff came in 2007 when Britons voted Aston Martin 'the coolest brand' – with the iPod only managing to squeak into second place ('Aston Martin tops cool brands list', *The Guardian*, 13 September 2007).

For the first handful of films, the cinematic Bond remains close to the literary template by wearing a Rolex Submariner wristwatch. This is replaced, rather disgracefully, by a Seiko model in *The Spy Who Loved Me* (1977) and for four subsequent films. Then, in *Goldeneye* (1996), Bond begins his current infatuation with Omega timepieces. The film also marks the debut of Bond's association with the Italian tailor Brioni. As costume designer

Lindy Hemming explained in an interview with *Time* magazine, this is not technically a product placement deal. 'I need 20 suits exactly the same for Bond but also the stand-ins, the stuntmen... I explained my dilemma, and [Brioni chief executive] Mr. [Umberto] Angeloni said, "I don't see any problem," and no money has changed hands' ('Measuring up', 8 May 2006).

Angeloni is to be congratulated for recognizing that the Bond seal approval equals money in the bank. As mentioned in Chapter 2, the recent movies bristle with product placement, from Bond's Persol sunglasses to his Sony VAIO laptop and his Sony Ericsson mobile phone. There's one jaw-dropping moment in *Casino Royale* when Bond actually tells his sultry companion that he's wearing an Omega watch. 'Beautiful,' she says. The Bond films have become so knowing that this could be perceived as an ironic commentary on their effectiveness as marketing juggernauts – a wink at today's brand-savvy consumers. Even so, the scene makes one squirm.

The cultural and sociological meaning of Bond has been analysed a thousand times, but there's no harm in re-stating the obvious truth that he is, perhaps, the perfect male role model. And with his addiction to premium brands, he is curiously more relevant to today's consumers than he was in the 1950s. Luxury has become democratized, so a slice of the Bond lifestyle is easier to obtain. How many male business travellers are subconsciously recreating a scene from a Bond movie when they step out onto the balcony of their hotel with a Smirnoff vodka and tonic in hand? And they can feel safe in the knowledge that nobody is watching them through a telescopic rifle sight.

BRANDING TOOLKIT

- The sports field is sacred.

- Fans readily accept sports sponsorship if it 'gives something back'.

- Soccer is the most popular televised sport worldwide – and its tribal characteristics greatly appeal to young men.

- For men in their late 20s and 30s, sport is a means of communication.

- Middle-aged men use TV sport to escape from their stressful lifestyles.

- They also use it as a way of bridging the generation gap.

- Men are discovering traditionally 'feminine' sports like yoga.

- Away from the sports field, action movies provide role models and product placement opportunities.

- TV product placement is still in its infancy.

11

Body

Inspired by the rugby game and a little daunted by the thought of the heavy meal ahead, he decides to hit the hotel gym for half an hour. He quickly changes into a T-shirt, shorts and Nike sports shoes and takes the lift down to the well-equipped fitness centre. He's no body-builder, but he definitely takes care of himself. He secretly despises middle-aged men who allow the pounds to pile on. The sight of a bulging beer gut inspires contempt – to him it represents laziness and lack of self-respect.

For a long time, he was a member of a chain of London fitness clubs called Holmes Place. More recently, though, he's joined a rather flashier gym in Soho called The Third Space. This would have cost him just over a thousand pounds a year, if the agency didn't pay half of it. Alongside all the usual weight training and cardio facilities it has a swimming pool (treated with ozone, so he doesn't come back from a lunchtime dip with red eyes), martial arts, yoga and a wide menu of health and wellbeing options, from acupuncture to osteopathy. Today, he considers, being fit goes hand in hand with being dynamic at work. A saggy body equals a saggy mind.

THE FITNESS IMPERATIVE

It's not enough to be healthy – you have to look the part. Thanks to the enthusiastic courting of the metrosexual by marketers, muscular bodies have become a familiar element of fashion and personal care advertising. An obvious example of this is the US brand Abercrombie & Fitch.

Once an upmarket outdoor sports equipment and apparel supplier – founded by Ezra Fitch and David Abercrombie in the early 20th century – the company began a slow decline in the 1960s. By 1988, when it was acquired by Limited Brands (the company, appropriately enough, behind lingerie brand Victoria's Secret), it was in a virtual coma. Its new owners solved the problem by aggressively re-launching it as a supplier of casual, vaguely outdoorsy fashion to college-age consumers. Today its stores are a bizarre combination of hunting lodge and nightclub, cluttered with deer antlers and suspended canoes and pumped with deafening rock music. Under-dressed and physically advantaged 'in-store models' take the place of conventional sales people.

In its stores, in its advertising and on its website, the brand uses extraordinary bodies to sell ordinary clothing. The strategy was best illustrated by a controversial magazine-style catalogue (or 'magalogue') that it published until 2003, featuring erotically charged photography by Bruce Weber. The approach is logical because Abercrombie & Fitch positions itself as a 'luxury casual wear' brand. As luxury implies inaccessibility, the barrier to entry here is created by physical appearance. A&F's marketing implies that imperfect people have no right to buy its products.

'Abercrombie & Fitch successfully resuscitated a 1990s version of a 1950s ideal – the white, masculine "beefcake" – during a time of political correctness and rejection of 50s orthodoxy. But it did so with profound and significant differences. A&F aged the masculine ideal downward, celebrating young men in their teens and early 20s with smooth, gym-toned bodies and perfectly coiffed hair. While feigning casualness... Abercrombie actually celebrates the vain, highly constructed male' ('The man behind Abercrombie & Fitch', Salon.com, 24 January 2006).

When the brand arrived in the UK at the beginning of 2007, much was made of the giant advertising posters depicting sculpted male torsos, and the unease they provoked among the average pallid, overweight men of the British Isles. The pressure was on to get back to the gym.

Historically speaking, gym culture is as old as the hills. The ancient Greeks felt that body and mind should be equally honed, and revered athletic physiques. The word gym derives from the Greek 'gumnos', meaning 'naked', and gymnasia were places where men dressed as nature intended to compete in races and boxing bouts. Unlike most modern gyms, these temples of physical perfection were also equipped with libraries to sharpen mental agility.

Modern attitudes to exercise, however, have their roots in the 19th century, when Christian values and 'clean thinking' were linked to healthy physical activity. In Britain, this manifested itself in the public school emphasis on sports and cold showers. In the United States, it spawned the Young Men's Christian Association (sing along now: YMCA), which was dedicated to 'The improvement of the spiritual, mental, social and physical condition of young men'. Many of its buildings contained swimming pools and recreation centres.

At this stage 'working out' still consisted of traditional sports or the lifting of free weights like dumbbells and barbells. We owe the look of today's typical fitness centre – with its formidable army of machines – to an eccentric adventurer named Arthur Jones, who died on 28 August 2007 at the age of 80.

Born in 1926 in Arkansas and raised in Oklahoma, Jones did a number of odd jobs before serving in the navy in the Second World War. Apart from exercise, his main enthusiasm in life was wild animals. He enjoyed big game hunting in Africa and started a business importing animals for zoos, transporting them in rickety B-52 bombers. In 1956 he made a film about trapping crocodiles in Africa. After this was aired on the ABC network he became a successful producer of action-packed wildlife films, making series with names like *Wild Cargo*, *Capture* and *Professional Hunter*. Married six times – always to women aged between 16 and 20 – his motto was 'Younger women, faster airplanes and bigger crocodiles'.

Perhaps in order to fully embrace these pursuits, Jones regularly worked out with weights. But he was frustrated by the results. 'I ended up with the arms and legs of a gorilla on the body of a spider monkey,' he contended ('Obituary: Arthur Jones', *The Times*, 1 September 2007). He began tinkering with weights and pulleys with the goal of producing a machine that worked muscle groups more efficiently. He discovered that if muscles were given time to recover, impressive results could be achieved with short but intense bursts of activity. In the late 1960s his experiments resulted in a prototype 'resistance' weight trainer called the Blue Monster. By simply removing and replacing a pin, users could now switch easily between heavier and lighter loads during a single session. Jones later marketed the machines under the name Nautilus, because the gears they depended on reminded him of nautilus seashells. Those who've used one of the things might come to the conclusion that the earlier name was more appropriate.

Sales of Nautilus machines made Jones one of the richest men in America: by the mid-1970s the company was earning US$300 million a year. Jones sold it for US$23 million in 1986 and bought a 600-acre site in Florida, which he turned into a vast private zoo with elephants, rhinos, gorillas and, of course, plenty of crocodiles. *The New York Times* commented: 'Mr. Jones' invention… helped to transform dank gyms filled with free weights and hulking men into fashionable fitness clubs popular with recreational athletes' ('Arthur Jones, 80, exercise machine inventor, dies', 30 August 2007).

Around the time that Jones was producing his first Nautilus machine, another fitness pioneer was devising a system that would speed the transformation of exercise into a lifestyle component. In 1968, doctor and former US Air Force health advisor Kenneth H. Cooper released a book called *Aerobics*. Instead of focusing on muscles, aerobics were concerned with the cardio-respiratory system: the heart, lungs and blood vessels. Walking, jogging and swimming are all aerobic forms of exercise. Cooper's next book, *The New Aerobics*, explained the system to a wider public and led to the music-driven exercise classes that took off in the 1980s, popularized by the actress Jane Fonda and her 'workout' videos. Like Nautilus machines, aerobics seemed to put athletic fitness within the reach of ordinary people.

These two ingredients gave rise to perfectly air-conditioned, sprung-floored, mirrored clubs that looked more like discos than conventional gyms. A new generation of young men and women had found an arena not only for exercising, but for preening, posing and flirting. In 1983, a journalist named Aaron Latham covered the hip Los Angeles gym scene in a *Rolling Stone* article headlined 'Looking for Mr Goodbody'. Two years later, the piece became the basis of the film *Perfect*, starring John Travolta as a journalist and Jamie Lee Curtis as an exercise coach.

In the success-obsessed eighties it was inevitable that physical perfection would become a goal. Gyms sprang up everywhere – from clean, well-lit places with modest membership fees to elite 'super-gyms', whose steep rates prevented overcrowding. The latter began to take on the characteristics of beauty parlours and health spas. By the 1990s they weren't even gyms any more, but establishments where you could become, by various means, a better person.

When the KX Gym (pronounced 'kicks') opened in London's Chelsea in 2002, it positioned itself as a 'five-star lifestyle experience'. In the reception area, the wood-panelled walls and the glass vases containing freshly cut lilies recalled a boutique hotel. Inside, as well as the usual equipment, KX offered Ayurvedic alternative health therapy from India and classes in Capoiera – Brazilian kickboxing. Its marketing encouraged clients to celebrate health, vitality, and themselves. The black and white photography on its website transformed exercise into art. Former banker Simon Fry, who founded the chain, said, 'All the gyms I had visited were very utilitarian. I wanted to create a five-star gym, with lots of decadent space. KX is a brand, like a perfume' ('Blood, sweat and rears', *The Independent*, 31 March 2002).

The marketing language used by premium clubs often incorporates spiritual and New Age elements. The Illoiha gym in Tokyo uses the slogan 'Fitness 1.618 relaxation'. This refers to the 'golden ratio', a number used in mathematics and the arts to represent forms with perfect balance. Through fitness programmes and spa treatments, members of the Illoiha club are invited to find their own perfect balance. Semi-mystical claims like this pepper the websites of today's gyms. How much they appeal to men is a moot point. Male baby boomers – still dragging around their spiritual hangover from the sixties – may buy into them. Otherwise, when they're not happily lifting weights, men are more likely to appreciate the martial arts option.

As they're essentially local services, the marketing of fitness clubs tends to favour word of mouth. Arranging press visits to generate media coverage is an obvious approach. Offering cut-rate corporate memberships to the business community is another. Conventional advertising is by no means out of the question, however.

Upmarket gym brand Equinox – which has about 40 clubs in cities across the United States – hired the advertising agency Fallon to consolidate its position as 'a luxury lifestyle brand'. Like other luxury brands, Equinox has developed links with celebrities, ensuring that a star is always on hand to open its latest branch. It has also stamped its logo on fitness products, apparel and juice bars. While the brand is positioned as young, it has an obvious appeal for stressed-out executives with an eye on their pulse rates. Health monitoring, personal achievement and customization are all underlined. New members are given a fitness assessment administered by 'an elite level fitness coach' to find out how healthy they are. They're then provided with a 'fully integrated fitness prescription' incorporating a range of services including strength training, cardio, group fitness, spa and nutrition. Fitness coaches have become the new gurus, somewhere between Obi Wan Kenobi from the *Star Wars* films and Morpheus in *The Matrix*.

With all this going on, staying fit is becoming a time-consuming task. For this reason, The Third Space in Soho is well-named. These clubs fill the void between home and office. Exercise there, get health advice there, eat, drink and socialize there – even get your laundry done there. It's like bolting the most convenient elements of a luxury hotel onto your daily life; with the added advantage that you get to sleep in your own bed. And as with loyalty schemes at hotels, the 'recognition' factor is important – members feel good when the receptionist greets them warmly by name.

As our obsession with health and appearance grows, we may require instant exercise fixes when the gym isn't close to hand. These are already available in Japan via Conbini fitness centres: minigyms that offer coin-operated workout facilities for impulse exercising. A ten-minute session costs the equivalent of a couple of dollars. Similar centres are likely to appear in airports, stations, launderettes and shopping malls across the world. Bringing an exercise element into previously leisurely pursuits is another option: 'sight jogging' is sightseeing undertaken at a brisk pace.

While gym-sculpted bodies have influenced fashion imagery, fitness technology is also inspiring retailers. For example, at The Third Space, those 'preparing to compete at altitude' can train on treadmills and exercise bikes in a 'hypoxic chamber', which reduces the quantity of circulating oxygen to mimic the thinner air at heights of 7,000 to 9,000 feet. Compare this to the Burton snowboarding equipment store in New York, where shoppers find out how the gear matches up to 'real' weather conditions in a 'cold room'. We'll see a lot of these test lab environments in stores, especially when the product is aimed at men – those keen consumers of functional apparel.

MAKING THE CUT

The urban male does not have to worry too much about necessities. The average day is eminently survivable, and food is literally handed to him on a plate. So he has plenty of time to dwell on the non-essential – his appearance, for example. But while advertising and glossy magazines encourage the pursuit of physical perfection, it's not always easy to catch. Even those who put in plenty of gym time find they have niggling faults that can't be corrected without help. Others are unwilling to succumb to the natural process of ageing. Many are turning to cosmetic surgery.

In fact, the number of cosmetic procedures performed on men in the US increased by 16 per cent between 2000 and 2005, according to the American Society of Plastic Surgeons. Another organization, the American Society of Aesthetic Plastic Surgery, adds that in the same year, 14 per cent of Botox injections, 15 per cent of all liposuction and eyelid surgeries, 20 per cent of laser hair removal and 24 per cent of nose jobs were carried out on men. In Britain, a 2006 survey by Sainsbury's Bank revealed that of the annual £5 million worth of loans that were being taken out for cosmetic surgery, one in five of them went to men.

And while they'd prefer not to talk about it, men aren't that difficult to sell to. Those who work in highly competitive sectors like banking and the media believe they are judged, at least partially, on their looks. Michael Atkinson, a sociology professor at McMaster University in Ontario, told *The Daily Telegraph*, 'One of the biggest drivers in cosmetic surgery is men of 40-plus who use this as a tool to look healthy, to look young. Traditionally, women have done cosmetic surgery to be competitive along beauty standards. Now men are doing that but for competition in the workplace. These guys are competing along lines of status and power in a market economy' ('New breed of young blade emerges', 4 March 2006).

But women may also drive male 'consumption' of cosmetic surgery procedures. Reports from the United States suggest that men who accompany their wives to consultations with surgeons often end up agreeing to the odd tweak themselves. The *Los Angeles Times* reported: 'In consultation rooms across the country, husbands who just come along for the ride are finding themselves on the business end of a scalpel... Others are trying to keep up with their partners, whose zeal for cosmetic improvement is making the men look old by comparison. Being mistakenly referred to as your wife's father is apparently quite the motivation' ('New you? New us', 10 April 2006). The men are in a poor position to complain about this state of affairs – after all, it's unlikely that they were initially attracted to their wives' minds.

One of the most brutally honest reports on the male cosmetic surgery trend was provided by a British journalist named Steve Beale, who described his own experiences in the *Evening Standard* ('Mr Nip and Tuck', 11 November 2005). Beale decided to go under the knife after years of struggling to come to terms with a condition called *gynecomastia* – or 'man breasts'. Although this affects about 10 per cent of men, and is thought to be genetic, Beale was weary of the draining effect it had on his self-confidence. He wrote: 'The truth is that in the early 21st century, medical science can get me more love, more sex, more self-esteem and better service in restaurants. It can even get me more work. In the age of pretty boys like David Beckham and Jude Law, the male form, for better or worse, is as closely scrutinised as the female form.'

It's perhaps fortunate that the industries in which good looks are considered important often provide the salaries – or the influence – that make improvement more accessible. So Beale strapped himself in not only to have his 'man breasts' removed, but also to have liposuction, Botox anti-wrinkle treatment, a bit of laser surgery on some back hair, and dental veneers. 'It's getting to the stage where we all know of someone who's had cosmetic surgery. I was encouraged to have my procedures by a close friend who'd already undergone similar ones… Of course I'd prefer to live in a world where I, and everyone else, ignored my physical defects. But I don't. And more and more men agree with me. In fact, 35 per cent of the patients at the established Harley Medical Group's network of cosmetic surgeries are male.'

For the time being, men don't generally have surgery to enhance their looks. The vast majority of them ignore the spam emails promising larger penises. What they want is to correct faults – the bump on the nose, the love handles, the sticky-out ears or, yes, the womanly breasts. But this, too, is changing. The American Society of Aesthetic Plastic Surgery says that procedures to create 'six pack abs' and 'bulging pecs' (abdominal and pectoral implants) and even buttock enhancements are becoming more popular.

One day, of course, there may be a trend for 'authentic' looks – rather like the current trend for vintage clothing. Yet it seems doubtful that men will be able to resist the pressure – from peers, from partners, from the media – to iron out faults and march confidently into a thinner, younger-looking future. Some of you belong to the last generation of men who will go through their entire lives without recourse to cosmetic enhancement.

BRANDING TOOLKIT

■ The male body is under more scrutiny than ever before.

■ 'Out of shape' is less acceptable socially and profession-
ally.

■ Male gym membership and cosmetic surgery are on the
rise.

■ Looking 'youthful' and avoiding heart disease are powerful motivators.

■ Elite clubs provide a 'third place' to relax between work
and home.

■ They are less about pure fitness than about overall self-
improvement.

■ Gym culture and 'stress test' experiences are finding
their way into retail environments.

12

Alcohol

Scene Twelve: L'Alcazar restaurant, Paris

He's cut down considerably on his alcohol intake since the hazy, beery days of his twenties. He now considers it an occasional treat, along with red meat and rich desserts. Although he'll still order a beer in a pub, these days he prefers a glass of wine, a good single malt whisky – or the drink that the waiter has just set down in front of him. In his opinion, few things provide better compensation for the hardships of life than a well-made dry martini. Contained in a real martini glass – just the kind that Sinatra might have sipped from – made with Bombay Sapphire and just a rumour of vermouth, perfectly chilled, with a bright comma of lemon peel sitting in the bottom. The drink is made even more enjoyable by the surroundings and the company. Sandrine has come alone: her boss is unavoidably detained by family matters.

He's pleased to note that she has ordered a glass of champagne. This isn't, then, going to be one of those rigid 'work talk' evenings during which he's forced to clamp whitening knuckles around a glass of mineral water. He's already looking forward to scanning the wine list.

Sandrine raises her glass. '*A votre santé.*'

'To your health, too,' he replies. Although he doubts the evening is going to do them much good in that respect.

THE BEER PUNTERS

Alcohol marketing is almost uniformly masculine in tone. The logic here is the same as it is for cars: women are not necessarily offended by an alcohol brand with masculine values, but men will never touch a drink with feminine associations. Among the rare products obviously aimed at women are 'alcopops' – the sweet-tasting potions like Bacardi Breezer that attained a peak of popularity in the 1990s, but were criticized by pressure groups and the media because they allegedly encouraged underage drinking.

While it has not been quite as demonized as tobacco, alcohol faces heavy advertising restrictions around the world. The European Union has devised a cross-border directive specifying, among other things, that alcohol promotion must not be aimed at minors, it must not link alcohol to 'social or sexual success', and it must not encourage 'immoderate consumption'. In the UK, alcohol advertising is regulated by the Advertising Standards Authority and, to a certain extent, by the industry itself. The United States has also opted for the self-regulatory path. Yet plenty of advertising still appears. And in both Europe and the United States, sponsorship of sports by alcohol brands is common. At the beginning of 2008 Coors Light began a five-year, US$20 million association with 'family-friendly' sport NASCAR. The deal gave the brand exclusive access to use the organization's logos in advertising, packaging and promotions, as well as sponsorship of the Pole Award, the prize for the fastest-qualifying time in each race.

Philip Almond, marketing director of drinks giant Diageo in the UK (whose brands include Smirnoff, Johnnie Walker, Guinness, Gordon's Gin and Dom Pérignon), says, 'Advertising regulations are getting tighter, but as far as Diageo is concerned, our internal marketing code is just as tough, if not tougher, than many local codes. What we've found is that restrictions tend to bring out more creativity. This is fortunate, as we're moving rapidly away from the 1950s world of 30 second TV commercials to a more experimental, permission-based system.'

Nevertheless, one of Diageo's key brands, Guinness, has benefited from a lengthy partnership with the London advertising agency AMV.BBDO. The agency has produced some of the most popular and striking alcohol commercials of recent years. For some time now the spots have used the same tagline: 'Good things come to those who wait.' As any Guinness drinker knows, pouring a pint of the black stuff is a lengthy affair. Remember the 'Surfer' spot from 1999, featuring white horses rearing out of the pounding waves? The surfers, who spend a lot of time anticipating the right wave, were an ideal metaphor for patience. But the film was also chock-full of mythic masculine imagery, from the rugged faces and taut sinews of the surfers to the dramatic voiceover, torn from the pages of *Moby Dick*.

'Guinness drinkers see themselves as a cut above lager drinkers,' says Almond, explaining the brew's brand profile. 'They think of it as a drink of substance. They're more sophisticated, more controlled, more mature.' And more manly? 'Interestingly enough, research has shown that men physiologically prefer a bitter taste,' he acknowledges.

Guinness and AMV.BBDO won the Grand Prix at the Cannes Lions International Advertising Festival – the equivalent of the film industry's annual bash – in 2006 with another TV spot called 'Noitulove' ('evolution' spelt backwards). It showed three men at a bar sipping pints of Guinness. Suddenly the action froze and the film went into reverse. The men walked backwards out of the bar and back through the evolutionary chain, devolving as they went. Finally, they ended up as mudskippers supping primordial soup. With its mind-boggling effects and jazzy Sammy Davis Junior soundtrack, the ad was a perfect example of 'advertainment'. But it was also a sophisticated version of the 'three guys in a bar' form of beer advertising. There's an oft-cited rule concerning booze ads. A man alone equals a potentially alcoholic loner. Two men: possibly gay. Three men, though, are buddies out on the town.

'The bar occupies an important social role in male culture,' says Almond. 'Think of the ritual of the round of drinks and the scorn that's reserved for blokes who don't "get their round in". But like bars themselves, I think drinks advertising is moving away from this sexual stereotyping and turning its attention to mixed group occasions. In the UK, the change in licensing laws has enabled bars to stay open later, which encourages a more relaxed, mid-tempo approach. The positioning of brands will reflect that change.'

It's fair to say, though, that the best known alcohol advertising campaigns were devised with guys in mind. Take Budweiser, for example: a solidly masculine brand. Having been brewed since 1876, Budweiser became the best-selling beer in the United States in 1957 – a title it has yet to relinquish. For years it was marketed under the slogan 'The King of Beers', succeeded in the 1970s by 'When you've said Budweiser, you've said it all', and then in the eighties by 'This Bud's for you'. By the early 1990s, however, market share was declining as a new generation turned their back on the beer, associating it with their dads. The brand returned to form in 1995 with the introduction of three animated Budweiser frogs, who in TV and online ads croaked 'Bud', 'weis', 'er' – to the growing irritation of a mobster-voiced onlooker, Louie the Lizard. The hapless Louie's antics as he tried to do away with the frogs were immensely popular.

Not as popular, however, as the next campaign: 'Wassup!?' The ads could not have been simpler: a group of young guys constantly greet each other with the word 'Wassup!?' uttered in exaggerated and comical tones. The creator of the films, Charles Stone III, had been doing the same thing with his own group of buddies for years. The atmosphere of male camaraderie – in which the pointless running joke expressed unspoken depths of warmth, affection and group identification – strongly appealed to consumers. Inevitably, the catchphrase entered popular culture.

It wasn't the first time the brand had put its finger on a truth about male bonding. When Budweiser owner Anheuser-Busch wanted to reinvigorate its reduced-calorie Bud Light brand, it sought a campaign that appealed to men, without alienating women. The first spot, in 1995, showed a young man out fishing with his father. Suddenly, the son turned and said, 'Dad. Well, you're my dad. And I love you, man.' His father replied calmly, 'You're not getting my Bud Light, Johnny.' The emotional beginning of the ad and its deadpan payoff spoke to young male consumers who 'got' the irony. It was the kind of ad they would have made for themselves.

But there was something else going on. David Mehar of the agency DDB Needham, who came up with the ad, said he based the idea on his own relationship with his father. 'This is how guys say, "I love you", with a little disclaimer,' he observed. Once again, the phrase was enthusiastically taken up by consumers and the media. One consumer confirmed, 'I have definitely said "I love you, man" to my friends' (Encyclopaedia of Major Marketing Campaigns, Volume 2, 2007, WARC). And so a beer ad freed certain young men from inhibition about expressing their emotions.

Other brands have pandered more blatantly to the male bonding instinct. In 2006, the beer brand Miller Lite and its advertising agency Crispin Porter & Bogusky came up with a campaign called 'Man Laws'. This featured a group of unreconstructed males discussing behaviour that was irrefutably masculine, officiated by Burt Reynolds. Subjects included the length of time a man should wait before hitting on his best friend's ex-girlfriend (six months, apparently). Although it was clearly devised to take advantage of the 'menaissance' trend, the campaign did not have a positive effect on sales, and was dropped ('Miller repeals "Man Law"', *Advertising Age*, 22 January 2007). Perhaps it was a little too retro for its intended audience: some of the Man Laws bordered on the offensive. Even so, a screed of protests in support of the campaign appeared on blogs, hinting that the Man Laws would achieve a kind of immortality online.

As if to underline Almond's theory about the shift toward the 'permission marketing' of alcohol brands, Anheuser-Busch launched an online entertainment channel called Bud TV in 2006. By providing their birth date and zip code in return for a password, visitors could access a YouTube-like selection of sketches and user-generated entertainment. Less than a year later, *Advertising Age* published figures from TNS Media Intelligence confirming that America's top brewers had cut spending on 'measured media' by 12 per cent, or US$131 million. Not only that, but sales had increased at the same time. The brewers said they had invested the missing millions – and more besides – in promotional events. These ranged from rock concerts to, in the case of Miller High Life, the 'Olympics of bar games' in Chicago.

Today's alcohol marketing uses 'a smattering of print and online advertising to fuel a wide array of promotional events' ('Big brewers gut ad spend, sell more beer', 24 September 2007). Rather than waiting to be outlawed from traditional media altogether – like tobacco brands – alcohol marketers have changed tack.

MARKETING THE HARD STUFF

The main challenge facing the marketers of hard liquor is to encourage its uptake among younger consumers, who may feel nervous – for reasons of price, taste or habit – about switching from beer. Perhaps the biggest barrier, in many markets, is faced by whisky. 'We've had considerable success in some parts of Europe, where whisky is considered an active, sociable drink. In Spain, for example, J & B became a trendy brand,' says Diageo's Philip Almond. 'In the UK, on the other hand, a consumer under the age of 35 tends to consider blended whisky his father's drink. It's something his dad might order after a round of golf. When younger drinkers order spirits, they tend to prefer vodka or American brands like Jack Daniel's, which has benefited from its links to mad axeman-type guitarists.'

Interestingly, Jack Daniel's associations with rock-and-roll excess are purely serendipitous: beyond the placing of posters at the occasional biker rally, it has rarely pushed this idea overtly. Instead, the world's top-selling American whiskey – which celebrated its 50th anniversary in 2004 – has focused on one of the brand values most favoured by men: authenticity.

One certainly can't accuse Jack Daniel's of being disloyal. It has essentially used the same advertising agency since 1954, when it hired a St Louis shop called Gardner Advertising. Just over ten years later, a young copywriter named Ted Simmons began working on the brand. Simmons eventually left to start his own agency, which was snapped up by a bigger outfit named Arnold Worldwide. At the time of writing, the Jack Daniel's account is still with Arnold.

Simmons told *The Advertiser*, 'The role of our advertising since the beginning was not to "sell whiskey" as much as it has been to communicate the story of the brand' ('Jack Daniel's Tennessee whiskey celebrates 50 years of advertising success', December 2004). In more than a thousand different ads, the brand's employees at Lynchburg, Tennessee have been portrayed as craftsmen who put a great deal of time, effort and (yes, folks) *love* into the distilling of whisky.

'On my first visit to Lynchburg, I found a very small town of old families and flowered front porches, a hardware store, a coffee shop, and a town square surrounded by old wooden benches,' Simmon recalled. 'To me, Lynchburg was a lot like baseball — wholesome, rooted in the past, a place of continuity where people had been doing the same thing for almost 150 years... The town and the people reflect an older, simpler, prouder time in America... The people of Lynchburg who appeared in many of the ads – those who work at the distillery, gather at the hardware store, or drink coffee at the Iron Kettle Cafe – helped create a strong connection between the brand and our consumers.'

One of the brand's strengths has been its devotion to an increasingly outmoded form of advertising: the copy-heavy print ad. Its research showed long ago that people waiting on the platform at underground stations never quite know what to do with themselves in the few short minutes before their train arrives. They don't talk to strangers, their newspapers get ruffled by the draft, and there's not enough time to get lost in the world of a novel. And so they read cross-track advertising. Can there be anyone in London who hasn't read at least one of Jack Daniel's ads while waiting for the Tube? Half the city must know that the stuff is 'charcoal-mellowed'.

Recently, Arnold Worldwide wanted to reactivate the brand by 'connecting with 21- to 34-year-old males' (surprise!) while 'retaining the older, core loyalists' (www.arnoldworldwide.com). As JD is now a global brand, the agency conducted research on six continents to find out what these consumers had in common. 'We learned that brands of alcohol men drink are "badges". Each brand makes a statement about how a man views himself, whether you're talking to guys in Paris, Texas or Paris, France. Further, from the bars of Chicago to the pubs of London we found Jack Daniel's unifying mindset: Jack Daniel's drinkers see themselves as "the man among men".'

The words and phrases they used to describe the brand included 'masculinity', 'quiet confidence', 'knowing smile', 'pride', 'trust', and 'genuine'. The resulting campaign was more or less a continuation of what had gone before. One of the print ads read: 'Enjoyed in fine establishments and questionable joints everywhere.' A film version showed a car driving through a sleepy Tennessee town. The voiceover said: 'You can find Jack Daniel's in 135 different countries – but every drop comes from a town with just one stop light.' Timeless, rugged, unpretentious, with a wry sense of humour: it's almost a template for marketing to men.

Other alcohol brands have benefited from a strong heritage. Vodka brand Smirnoff sensibly plays on its Russian roots. The brand was created in 1850 by Pyotr Arsenyevitch Smirnov, who later passed the distillery to his sons, Vladimir and Nicolai. During the Russian revolution, the distillery was confiscated by the state and the Smirnovs were arrested. Nicolai died in prison, but Vladimir managed to escape during a short-lived counter-revolution. He re-established the Smirnov distillery in France under the westernized name Smirnoff. In 1933, he sold the brand to Rudolph Kunett, a Russian émigré living in the United States. At that stage, however, Eastern European expatriates were about the only people who would touch vodka. Kunett eventually relinquished the brand to another US distillery, Heublein. And here's where a bit of branding genius comes into play.

Soon after Heublein had acquired the brand, a labelling error resulted in a crate of Smirnoff vodka being packaged as whisky. A light-bulb appeared over the head of the company's president, John Martin, who began to market the drink as 'Smirnoff's white whisky'. The label added: 'No taste. No smell.' In a society still conflicted about imbibing in the wake of the Prohibition, these were powerful selling points. It also helped that vodka turned out to be the perfect cocktail ingredient. Martin proved that beyond a doubt when he teamed up with Hollywood restaurateur Jack Morgan, importer of an obscure British drink called ginger beer. Smirnoff and ginger beer together, topped off with a twist of lime, became the Moscow Mule. Suddenly, vodka was fashionable.

Politics aided Smirnoff during the Cold War, when Russia stopped exporting vodka to the West. The brand found itself with a monopoly on what became one of the most popular cocktail ingredients of the sixties. Notably, it was the choice of that most obliging of brand champions, James Bond, who required it to make his vodka martinis. Smirnoff has benefited from the association ever since.

Today, the brand is owned by Diageo. 'The dramatic story of the brand's journey from Russia appeals to consumers,' says Philip Almond. 'Male consumers, particularly, like their brands to have underpinnings of heritage and solidarity. They'll go for something fly-by-night for a while, but not for long. They appreciate classic brands.'

Classic brands, though, can be manufactured. Look at the success of Absolut, which until the 1980s was just an obscure vodka brand from Sweden – not even from Russia, for goodness' sake. Absolut was transformed into a cult tipple by the advertising agency TBWA and the brand's American importers, Carillon. The advertising turned one of Absolut's perceived negatives – its oddly-shaped bottle – into an attribute. Its print ads made the product the star. No beautiful people, no VIPs, just the bottle and a punning headline, such as 'Absolut perfection'. The bottle-as-logo approach meant that Absolut would become one of the most recognizable brands in the world. Carillon then placed the peculiar bottles in New York's trendiest nightclubs and bars. The brand's ascent to modishness was completed when Carillon convinced contemporary artists like Keith Haring and Andy Warhol to design some of its ads. Even today, Absolut retains its elitist, avant-garde air.

The man who masterminded the Absolut campaign was Carillon's boss, an energetic expatriate Frenchman named Michel Roux. But Roux wasn't finished yet. Having turned Swedish vodka into one of the most fashionable drinks on the planet, he then set out to drag gin from the doldrums.

At that stage – we're in 1988 – gin was almost as negatively per-ceived as it had been in the days when it was called 'mother's ruin', which hardly recommended it to the nightclub set. It had been derived from a sixteenth century Dutch concoction called *genever*, made with grain, juniper berries, herbs and spices – the original 'Dutch courage'. This was enthusiastically adopted by the British, who transformed it over a couple of centuries from distinctly dodgy firewater into a clean, clear, unsweetened drink with subtle botanical flavourings: the drink known as London Dry Gin.

The category enjoyed a golden era in the 1950s, when it was the basis for the original Dry Martini. But its thunder was stolen by a flashy newcomer called vodka, and by the 1980s gin definitely seemed like a poor *boisson*. Its unmistakable, juniper-driven taste compared unfavourably with the blander, mix-friendly vodka. 'It has often been a criticism of gin that its prime power base is the older middle to upper-class consumer – dubbed in the UK the Gin & Jag brigade,' explained trade journal *Drinks International*. 'With a higher disposable income, these consumers are prepared to pay the extra for premium gins. But, at the same time, this has given gin almost a fuddy-duddy image and, as a result, the category has traditionally failed to attract the younger emerging consumer, leaving the door wide open to vodka' ('Bombay mix is a modern-day hit', 1 May 2007).

At Carillon, Michel Roux was trying to kick some life into a gin called Bombay. In 1988 he launched a premium product called Bombay Sapphire, which had a subtler flavour than many of its rivals, with less of a juniper bite and more of an accent on the botanicals: almonds, lemon, liquorice, angelica and coriander among them. This was packaged in a rather gorgeous pale blue bottle – Roux understood the competitive advantage of a distinctive bottle – with a portrait of Queen Victoria on the side above the words 'from a 1761 recipe'. A classic had been born, almost overnight.

But the brand-friendly protagonist who introduces each chapter of this book favours Bombay Sapphire for quite another reason. He works for a design and branding agency – and Bombay Sapphire has developed strong links with the world of design. When the brand was launched, Carillon commissioned leading designers to come up with new interpretations of the martini glass. Print advertising featured these creations alongside the striking Bombay bottle, with the line, 'Pour something priceless'. In addition, consumers could buy the designer martini glasses with a bottle of Bombay Sapphire as part of a gift pack ('Michel Roux: blithe spirit', *Brandweek*, 12 October 1998).

Today owned by Bacardi-Martini, the brand retains close associations with the design community through its Bombay Sapphire Foundation. This runs two annual competitions: the Bombay Sapphire Designer Glass Competition, inspired by those original ads; and the Bombay Sapphire Prize, which recognizes original designs or artworks using glass. On the foundation's board are design gurus such as Ron Arad, Tom Dixon and Thomas Heatherwick.

The result of all this is that – just as Michel Roux intended – Bombay Sapphire is one of the hippest brands behind the bar. It also gave a boost to the entire gin category. Global brand director Andrew Carter told *Drinks International*: 'Bombay Sapphire… has rewritten the rule book thanks to its subtle yet complex taste and its striking blue bottle. As a result, Bombay Sapphire has successfully attracted a whole new audience to the gin category and we are continuing to recruit new consumers from outside the traditional boundaries of the market.'

THE HEALTH DEBATE

Men drink more than women. According to the World Health Organization, Europe has the world's highest consumption of alcohol, with adults consuming on average 12.1 litres of pure alcohol per person per year (2005) – more than twice the global level of 5.8 litres. Women only account for between 20 and 30 per cent of overall consumption. Meanwhile, the National Health Service in the UK reports that 34 per cent of men drink more than the recommended daily four units at least once a week, as opposed to 20 per cent of women. And in the United States, the National Institute on Alcohol Abuse and Alcoholism agrees that alcohol consumption is more prevalent among men than women.

What does this mean for men? Logically speaking, it means that we are more exposed to diseases such as cirrhosis of the liver, as well as the 'risky behaviour' associated with drinking – everything from getting into a bar fight to failing to turn up for an important meeting the next day, with subsequent crippling effects on our careers. And God forbid that we should get behind the wheel of a car. Not only that, but numerous surveys show that men feel they suffer from more stress than women – and in many male cultures, a night out drinking with the lads is an acceptable way of relaxing.

On the other hand, while there's no question that heavy drinking puts men at risk from various health problems, there is increasing evidence that moderate drinking may actually benefit them. We've all heard the theory that a drink or two a day – especially red wine – may offer protection from cardiovascular disease, as it plays a mine-sweeping role within clogged arteries. Research conducted by, once again, the National Institute on Alcohol Abuse and Alcoholism shows that the stats on alcohol consumption and health form a 'U' shape. At one end of the U are the abstainers, who seem to be vulnerable to illness even though they've never touched a drop in their lives – while at the other end are the alcohol abusers. Sitting smugly at the bottom of the U, with the lowest rates of death 'from all causes', are moderate drinkers (Health Risks and Benefits of Alcohol Consumption, NIAA, 2000).

A team of Italian university researchers made headlines in 2006 when it supported these claims. Based on pooled data from 34 large studies involving more than one million people and 94,000 deaths, they came to the conclusion that drinking moderately reduces the risk of death from any cause by roughly 18 per cent. Dr Augusto Di Castelnuovo, from the Catholic University of Campobasso, said in a statement that because men and women metabolize alcohol differently, the maximum dosage for men was four glasses a day – while women should stick to two. After that, though, it was all good news. Drink as a feature of the Mediterranean diet – a glass or two with dinner – could be considered part of a healthy lifestyle (Reuters, 12 December 2006).

Elsewhere, studies have shown that moderate alcohol consumption may protect against Alzheimer's and improve cognitive ability. These surveys should be taken rather like a glass of tequila – with a pinch of salt – but they no doubt give alcohol marketers cause to rejoice. Following the slump in sales of 'alcopops', could the next generation of alcoholic drinks spin some kind of health claim into their positioning? Advertising restrictions forbid marketers to make 'performance' claims for alcoholic drinks – but packaging can be suggestive. And as we've heard, the drinks companies are slowly shifting their budgets online. The Wild Web is the ideal terrain for planting new ideas.

BRANDING TOOLKIT

■ Men drink more than women.

■ Drinking is an important part of the male bonding ritual.

■ Men treat their favourite drinks as 'badges' of identity and status.

■ They prefer classic, down-to-earth brands with a strong heritage.

■ Packaging – the bottle – and point-of-sale marketing are important.

■ 'Fly-by-night' or trendy drinks may be sampled, but are quickly dismissed.

- Increasing alcohol advertising restrictions are forcing brands online.

- Sponsorship of sporting events remains heavy.

- The idea that moderate drinking has health benefits is gaining acceptance.

13

Restaurants

Scene Thirteen: L'Alcazar restaurant, Paris

'Restaurants are the new nightclubs,' one of his friends told him, and he had to agree. He'd prefer to cook for himself than consume bad food in bland surroundings. He considers eating out a form of entertainment. The restaurant he's currently sitting in suits him nicely. In many ways it is a classic Parisian *brasserie*: the long room lined with banquettes; the tables within cosy proximity of one another. But here the banquettes are upholstered in plum-coloured velvet, the white tablecloths gleam purposefully, and the waiters have youthful haircuts. The steaming, bustling kitchen is visible through a glass partition. The music is unobtrusive but contemporary electro (L'Alcazar, too, has its own compilation CD). There's a tangible effort to create a feeling of excitement.

He looks down at the menu, wondering whether to throw caution to the wind and order *foie gras* (with '*chutney de pommes*', no less!) as a starter despite its potentially deleterious effects on his waistline. He could always follow up with fish for the main course. What was the point of staying healthy if you couldn't indulge yourself from time to time?

'I'll take the salmon *en entrée*,' says Sandrine, who clearly doesn't agree with this strategy.

RESTAURANTS AS BRANDS

L'Alcazar in Paris is one of a global chain of luxury restaurants owned by a company called D&D London. Run by David Loewi and Des Gunewardena, in September 2006 D&D took over the establishments formerly run by Conran Restaurants. Before that, Gunewardena had worked for Sir Terence Conran for 17 years, observing at first hand how Conran made dining part of the entertainment industry. With his uncanny knack for nurturing lifestyle trends (see Chapter 4) Conran introduced the British to the European concept of the restaurant as focal point for a night out, as opposed to the pub or nightclub. One of the accelerators of this transformation was a *brasserie*-style restaurant called Quaglino's, which opened in London's St James's in 1993. Big, noisy and theatrical, with a sweeping staircase and statuesque cigarette girls, as well as mountainous platters of seafood, it demonstrated that a restaurant could be an experience. Diners were so enraptured that some of them stole the distinctive Q-shaped ashtrays as souvenirs.

'Everyone said we were mad,' Gunewardena told the *Evening Standard*. 'It was twice as big as Langan's, which at the time was the biggest restaurant in London, and it was in the teeth of the recession. But it was an amazing success. We planned to do £5 million turnover that first year, and, in fact, we did £10 million.' ('It's not Terry's, it's ours', 16 March 2007.)

The same dubious mutterings greeted the opening of La Pont de la Tour, near Tower Bridge. '[I]t was on the wrong side of the river, a taxi-ride away. It's a funny thing about restaurants, but the fact that one is slightly more difficult to get to can add to the allure of it,' Gunewardena explained.

The dockside former warehouses of Butler's Wharf, where La Pont de la Tour was located, eventually evolved into what Conran termed a 'gastrodrome': a full range of gastronomic options including restaurants, a café, food retailers, a wine merchant and a bakery. D&D has since opened a similar operation, The Customs House, in Copenhagen. The company also has restaurants in New York and Tokyo, with more to come.

From the beginning, certain elements of Conran – now D&D – establishments revealed the company's knack for branding. Each had a distinctive logo, which found its way onto match-folders and those desirable ashtrays. The décor tended to be similar: the minimalist yet luxurious design, the exposed kitchens. The restaurants came with buzzing bar scenes attached, ramping up the sense of occasion and telegraphing the idea that this was 'the place to be'. Media coverage was conspicuous. Since then, those restaurants in the group that were thought to have lost their edge have been 'rebranded'. Such was the case with a restaurant called Mezzo in London's Soho. Once fashionable, it had begun to blend in to the landscape. So D&D transformed it into a colourful Cuban joint called Floridita, which appeals to the area's young media crowd.

Times have changed since critics muttered darkly about the 'Conranization' of the London dining scene: now every restaurant owner dreams of creating a destination brand.

D&D's sales and marketing director is Judith Speller, who previously worked at hotel groups such as Hand Picked Hotels and Le Meridien. She has great experience in dealing with expense account customers – and business people entertaining their clients form a core part of any luxury restaurant's clientele. 'The key there is definitely service,' she said. 'It has to be slick, efficient and practically invisible. The business guest doesn't want to spend much time consulting the menu and ordering. As soon as the waiter has come and gone, he's forgotten the brief interruption and has launched straight back into his conversation.'

In the quest for faultless service, restaurants tend to stage a two-week or ten day 'pre-opening' period, when they do little marketing and attempt to iron out any glitches that may occur.

Speller admits, however, that it's impossible to manage restaurant critics. 'As soon as any new restaurant opens, they're in like a shot,' she says. 'A report from a critic used to make or break a restaurant, but these days they aren't quite as powerful. People are likely to compare them with customer reviews on the internet. And even restaurant guides often include a variety of comments from readers.'

Speller confirms that PR is 'massively important' for the restaurant trade. 'The question is: how do you attract press coverage when you own a restaurant that's already 15 or 20 years old? You can do that with promotional offers or discounts, but as a luxury brand that might not necessarily be the way to go. You can create events around key dates or anniversaries. Some restaurateurs and barmen write regular columns in newspapers.'

We've mentioned the lure of the 'celebrity chef' before. In many ways this is the ultimate marketing gimmick, as the chef one sees every week on television is unlikely to be giving orders in the kitchen when you dine at his restaurant. Other minor celebrities may be sprinkled around the dining room, however, which helps a restaurant's notoriety no end.

Some restaurants become part of a 'scene' – whether real or imagined. Journalists love this idea, as they're always looking for the modern equivalent of Dorothy Parker's famous 'round table' at the Algonquin Hotel in 1920s New York, where writers would sling witticisms instead of bread rolls. 'Scene' restaurants in London over the years have included the Soho Brasserie in the 1980s and the Atlantic Bar & Grill in the 1990s. The latter was opened in 1994 by a young restaurateur called Oliver Peyton. It was located in the formerly disused basement of the Regent Palace Hotel, just off Piccadilly Circus, which Peyton restored to its former art deco glory. Guests had the impression they were dining in an ocean liner. For a while it was a genuine phenomenon: well-heeled young things queued around the block to get in. Peyton – who still owns a string of luxury restaurants – revealed the secret of its success to *The Observer* newspaper. 'I got really fed up with that British pomposity and not getting proper service unless you were dressed in a particular way. Restaurants should be classless places, where people who are earning money can have a good time – it's quite difficult to have a good time in England, especially in the winter.' Peyton's mantra is simply that 'restaurants should be fun'. The newspaper called him 'an impresario of pleasure' ('Peyton's place', 16 June 2002).

The New York equivalent might be Odeon, in Tribeca, which author Jay McInerney immortalized as the apex of the downtown scene in his 1984 yuppie redemption novel *Bright Lights, Big City*. McInerney described the restaurant as 'glittering' and 'curvilinear' with 'good light and clean luncheonette-via-Cartier deco décor'. It was owned by a couple of English brothers called Brian and Keith McNally. When he'd completed his book, McInerney asked their permission to use the restaurant's façade on the cover, even if 'the novel contained a scene in which the protagonist snorted coke in the restaurant's toilets'. The brothers agreed, not entirely convinced the book would ever see the light of day. Nine months later, Keith McNally found himself rooted in front of a bookstore window on Fifth Avenue. 'I saw a photograph of Odeon plastered all over the windows of this store…It was a bit like seeing an image of yourself, and not looking the way you think you look' ('A New York state of mind', *The Independent on Sunday*, 21 November 2004). Even today, the restaurant's frontage adorns the cover of the Vintage paperback – and Odeon is still going strong.

The fact that both the Soho Brasserie and the Atlantic Bar & Grill have long gone, however, stands as a warning that scenes move on. Longevity is hard to achieve without making constant changes – to the menu, to the décor – that might generate press coverage and prompt return visits. Speller says, 'The exception would be a Michelin-starred restaurant, which doesn't do much marketing at all.'

The first Michelin guide was published in 1900 by André Michelin of the French tyre-making family (the guide was given away with the purchase of a set of tyres). At that point it was merely a collection of tips for the first generation of automobile owners: where to find garages, doctors, hotels and 'curiosities' along the route. It was not until 1920 that the first restaurant reviews appeared, with the establishment of a complete star system (between one and three) in 1931. Just over 70 years later, *Le Guide Michelin* had become so influential that there were reports of chefs threatening suicide if they lost a star ('*Les blues des chefs*', *L'Express*, 15 May 2003). This has never happened, but in the rarefied world of gourmet restaurants, the Michelin inspectors still count.

GENEROUS TIPS

But how do more down-to-earth establishments cope in a sector that is, in Speller's words, 'enormously competitive'? As they're often communicating with people who live or work within a five mile radius, straightforward advertising is almost uniformly considered a waste of money. Direct marketing is a far more sensible approach. Restaurants with an organized approach to marketing keep databases of their customers – names, telephone numbers and, whenever possible, e-mail addresses. These can then be targeted with news of special offers and events. Bearing in mind that the restaurant itself plays the role of a billboard – encouraging potential customers to find out more about it – a website is obligatory. This should give the customer the opportunity to sign up for a newsletter. Restaurants also turn to list brokerage firms for addresses of consumers who've recently moved into the area; or credit card holders who describe themselves as 'frequent diners' in usage surveys.

Mail-outs to local companies are another obvious approach. In terms of events, free or cut-price 'tasting sessions' create customers: we all know the power of the 'happy hour'. Some restaurants establish a rapport with potential corporate clients by offering catering services for meetings. Others operate a 'value pricing' system, changing the price and contents of the menu to reflect economic fluctuations. When one restaurant in the financial district of New York heard that a major firm in the area had cut its employees' expense accounts by 30 per cent, it quickly brought out a new menu containing a wider range of moderately priced dishes. When their marketing has succeeded, restaurateurs do all they can to ensure that customers spend lavishly. Many of them put the most expensive items on the menu in the place where the average customer looks first: the top of the second page.

If all this sounds faintly desperate, let's consider what's at stake. In the two months after the terrorist attacks of 9/11, restaurant attendance in the United States dropped so sharply that the National Restaurant Association launched an advertising campaign in a bid to bring back customers. It used the slogan, 'Join us. Help America turn the tables.' The campaign cost US$5 million. Mere breadcrumbs, considering the restaurant trade had lost more than US$1 billion in just two months ('Looking for ways to get people back in the habit of having a night out', *New York Times*, 13 December 2001).

Of course, the restaurant business doesn't always act in accordance with its vulnerability. Poor service is endemic, and the male customer is often at the sharp end of it. That's because, despite protestations to the contrary, if a man and a woman are dining together it's very often the man who has reserved the table and will eventually pay the bill.

This situation has many disadvantages – not least for women, who say they are often treated as second-class citizens at restaurants. They believe that men are shown to better tables, are automatically presented with the wine list and receive more attention from the waiter – or, more to the point, the waitress. This is partly due to the fact that, in restaurant lore, men are said to be better tippers. Tim Zagat, compiler of the eponymous restaurant guide, confirmed that, at least in New York City, sexism in restaurants is far from uncommon ('Sexism is on the menu in many NY restaurants', *New York Post*, 28 February 2007).

Equality, though, has turned restaurants into behavioural mine-fields. When a woman suggests splitting the cost of a meal, does she mean it? Will he lose her respect if he accepts? Or will she consider him sexist if he insists on paying? For most men, the second possibility is the least alarming.

Alan Richman, the food writer and columnist at American *GQ*, wrote an excellent article called The Restaurant Commandments (July 2004), in which he skewered the heart of what was wrong with many restaurant experiences. Two of them strike a particular chord with men. The first is 'Don't banish us to the bar'. Richman writes: 'The all-too-common phrase "Your table isn't quite ready" invariably means the customer is sent off grumbling to a packed bar. Restaurants that can't honour reservations on time should offer some sort of consolation to inconvenienced guests, even if it's nothing more than a complimentary glass of the not-very-good house wine. People don't become customers the moment they're seated. They're customers as soon as they walk in the door.'

Men find this situation particularly offensive as it makes them feel as if they are a) not important enough or b) not in control of the situation. Either way, they suspect the waiter has blown their chances with their date and begin to resent the restaurant from that moment on. The other rule that seems to have been written specifically with men in mind is, 'Bring back the dress code'. Richman tells us, 'I'm sick of putting on a jacket to go out to dinner and finding myself surrounded by velour tracksuits.'

It's okay if restaurants are positioned as the new nightclubs, but we don't want them to resemble gyms.

BRANDING TOOLKIT

■ Restaurants are places of corporate or personal entertainment.

■ Men are often the main focus of attention from staff.

■ They want to feel important, knowledgeable and in control.

■ Business customers expect 'invisible' service.

■ PR and direct marketing are the most common marketing techniques.

■ Database management is extremely important.

■ The internet and e-mail have transformed restaurant marketing.

14

Sex

Scene Fourteen: Taxi interior, Paris

He holds open her pale cashmere overcoat and as she slips her arms into the sleeves he can smell her perfume. Towards the end of the meal, when the bottle of wine was almost empty, he noticed a faint blush appearing along her cheekbones. They've talked quite a lot about work, a little about themselves. There is definitely a mild flirtation going on.

He considers himself averagely experienced in these matters. He would describe himself as a serial monogamist: he's had a few relationships, but always fairly long-term and generally one at a time. In moments of drunken abandon he's usually had a condom to hand and quite often he's used it. He came of age in the late 1980s, surrounded by dramatic advertising about the threat of AIDS. These days, though, he doesn't consider himself at risk. He doesn't think he's ever met anyone with AIDS, or even anyone who's HIV positive. His girlfriend is on the pill and he hasn't used a condom for ages. He's never liked them (inconvenient and ugly, with their clinical foil packets) and he's not sure he could handle one now.

But let's not get ahead of ourselves. He holds the door open for her, because he believes that women still value these little touches of chivalry. Then they're outside in the fresh autumn air. He tells her he thinks there's a taxi rank beside the Metro station. Their situation remains unresolved because taxis are scarce and they're forced to share. She gives the driver her address. If this was a film he'd make some kind of move – at least put his hand on hers – but he does nothing. The glowing taxi radio is playing jazz, interrupted now and then by the crackling voice of the dispatcher.

They glide to a halt in a narrow street. She gets out. He follows but stands with one hand on the open door of the car. She is looking at him. 'So,' he says, by way of an explanation, 'I hope we'll soon be working together. Thanks for a great evening.'

She nods, slowly. 'Until next time, then.'

She allows herself to be kissed on each cheek. He watches her push open the heavy door of her apartment building, revealing a slice of cobbled courtyard beyond. Then he gets back into the taxi and tells the driver the name of his hotel. As the car accelerates down the street, he feels proud of his self-restraint. *Definitely up for it*, he reckons, with a trace of his old laddishness.

He looks at his watch. Then he reaches into the inside breast pocket of his coat, briefly revealing the Paul Smith label. He pulls out his new personal phone – the latest Motorola Razr. It's not too late to call his girlfriend. His concept of loyalty extends to more than mere brand names, after all.

INTERNET CONNECTIONS

Men are constantly bombarded with sexual imagery. Sex sells, as everyone knows, and plenty of advertisers still use female flesh to hook eyeballs. Inaccessible beauty in various states of undress sprawls across billboards, magazine racks and screens. Business travellers returning from extended trips to Saudi Arabia – where magazines like *GQ* are confiscated at the airport as pornography

– are shocked by the sudden realization that the urban landscape is a 24-hour prick-tease. Young men out for a night on the town are targeted by bands of pretty women taunting them with packs of cigarettes, branded lighters or free tequila shots. 'At clubs including The Back Room in Austin, Texas; Bottom of the Hill in San Francisco; and Churchill's in Miami, Zippo featured at least three glamorous young women dubbed "The Zippo Hotties" who collected the names and contact information of people wanting to compete in its "Wheel of Fire" on-site competition to win Zippo-related premiums' ('Marketers step out for drinks', *Advertising Age*, 19 January 2004).

Yet beneath this glossy veneer of titillation lies the complex reality of relationships. Young men desperate to hook up, older men afraid of commitment, mature men still looking for a partner, married men going through mid-life crises, divorced men thrown back into the glare of the dating circuit… the variations are as myriad as the challenges facing women.

The internet is a relatively new strand in the tangled web of human emotions. Less than 15 years ago, those who had given up on the conventional hunting grounds – work, bars, clubs, friends of friends – had to turn to classified advertising to look for a mate. In the late 1990s, however, websites offering a discreet alternative to small ads began to emerge. One such site was Match.com, launched in San Francisco in 1995 by the Internet pioneer Gary Kremen. Then 31 years old, Kremen had become convinced that classified advertising would shift onto the web. He later sold the service, making little out of the deal at the time, although he became rich through other Internet interests.

Match.com took a step forward when it acquired a Dallas-based rival called The One & Only Network. The Match brand was retained, powered by One & Only's superior technology. Headquartered in Dallas, Match.com is now the biggest online dating service in the world, with 15 million 'members' and 60,000 new users every day. It is owned by Internet conglomerate

InterActive Corp (IAC), headed by Barry Diller, which has more than 60 other brands including Ask.com and Ticketmaster. The Match.com website says the service has a simple mission: 'To take the lottery out of love.'

The brand's CEO is Thomas Enraght-Moony, a South African who studied history at Glasgow University, then for an MBA at INSEAD. He originally joined Match in 2004 to run its North American operations, rising to COO a year later and his current position in the spring of 2007. Immediately before arriving at Match, he was vice-president of e-commerce for AT&T Wireless. His background says something useful about Match.com – and about online dating in general. Virtual love is big business. Match. com brings in revenue of more than US$300 million a year for IAC.

Not that the company coldly regards relationships as a commodity – not outwardly, at least. Visitors to its headquarters report that the lobby 'looks like a slightly naughty boudoir, with velvet chaise longues, overstuffed chairs, crystal chandeliers and a staircase that could have come from the set of *Gone With The Wind*. The reception desk candy bowl is filled with Hershey's Kisses' ('Match.com picks its new Mr Right', *Dallas News*, 25 April 2007). Enraght-Moony sounds sincere when he says, 'What I enjoy about this job is the way that our technology has the power to change people's lives. It creates opportunities. It's an enabler of human relationships.'

The emergence of online dating was inevitable. One of the most seductive things about the internet is its sheer convenience. It simplifies a wide range of activities, from academic research to shopping. Dating is one other thing that the net has made a whole lot easier: why waste time trawling bars when you can look for a partner from the comfort of your own home – or your office? The web has also excised some of the most discomfiting elements of the dating ritual. Hitting on somebody in a bar takes a bit of pluck: chances are they're in a relationship or not interested in starting one, especially with you. On Match.com and its rival services, everybody knows what they are there for.

Once Match.com users have signed up for an account, they create a profile describing who they are and what they want. At the same time, they can use the system's complex 'matching technology' to look for people. The service has considered the fact that gifted writers have a natural advantage in the online dating world. Advisors are on hand to check profiles and lightly rewrite them, if only to correct the grammar. Beyond that, though, the 'conversations' that take place via the service reverse the usual evolution of relationships. The communication is 99 per cent written, meaning that daters know a great deal about one another before they ever meet. The downside is that it's far harder to tell when somebody is lying. Exchanging e-mails is great for bantering, but you can't really know a person until you've looked into their eyes.

Match.com does all it can to reduce the obvious dangers that come with such a situation. Extensive privacy controls are in place – including a 'double blind' e-mail system that means nobody can be contacted directly against their wishes. Members are advised to remain anonymous, to set up specific e-mail addresses for dating purposes, and never to provide personal contact details. The site also offers dating tips with a strong focus on security: 'Meeting offline? Think safety first!' If a single complaint is made about a member, they're banned from the site for life.

Realistically, Match.com has no more control than the owner of a nightclub over whether people use its service to seek casual flings or long-term partners. But Enraght-Moony says it can boast plenty of happy endings. He tells the story, for instance, of a woman who had her eye on a local fireman, but was too shy to talk to him. She went on Match.com and – click! – there he was.

By some accounts, our ease with the Internet has made online dating commonplace. 'In New York, Internet dating has become so prevalent that some women call it "man shopping" and "hyper-dating",' reported the *Financial Times*. 'Elsewhere, some people are apparently setting up more than 10 dates a week – and in some cases, several on one night' ('The silliness of online dating has been taken to new heights', 4 November 2005).

Enraght-Moony is less convinced. 'Attitudes have definitely changed, but one of our fundamental business challenges is to drive category acceptance. Five years ago, people wouldn't have felt comfortable admitting they met on Match.com – they'd probably say they met in a bar. Now they're much more willing to talk about it. But a lot of people still have a personal stigma about online dating. They might congratulate their friends, while secretly thinking that it's not for them. That's a tremendous business opportunity for us, because there are an estimated 92 million single people in the US alone.'

He denies that social networking sites like MySpace and Facebook – which encourage a fair amount of flirting – have eaten into his customer base. 'If anything they've made people feel more at ease with services like ours. We place advertising on those sites.'

Match.com's marketing runs the gamut of media opportunities – TV, print, radio and online – although Enraght-Moony says 'word of mouth and customer recommendation is still the most powerful form of promotion'. He adds that conventional advertising tends to be aimed at women, simply because men are more likely to use the site unprompted. 'I hope this doesn't sound too sexist, but in my experience dating in online world is the same as dating in the real world: men tend to be the chasers and women tend to be the chased. It's the men who initiate the conversation, just as they're expected to in bars. We try to encourage women to be proactive, as they'll be more successful that way, but at the end of the day people are people.'

Match.com operates sites in 35 countries and 15 languages, and the rules of engagement differ. 'In America, for example, which tends to be a car-bound culture, radio can be very effective. In the United Kingdom, it might be advertising on commuter trains or the London Underground. There's definitely not a one-size-fits-all approach.'

National cultures vary almost as widely as the people looking for love.

PERFORMANCE BLUES

Given the parade of gorgeous women and potent men that passes practically daily before our eyes, it's not surprising that the average male feels a little insecure. It is a convention in movies that the hero is rewarded for his courage with sex. This is invariably satisfying for both parties. Our *über*-hero, James Bond, has traversed film after film bedding pretty much any woman he chooses, without fear of rejection. But we know only too well that reality does not mirror this cinematic state of affairs. We are slaves to the caprices of our bodies, and women are not the obliging figures often depicted on the screen.

Younger men, particularly, have problems dealing with this contrast. They worry that, once they have convinced a woman to sleep with them in the first place, they may not be able to deliver a performance worthy of Hollywood. The drug sildenafil – best known under the brand name Viagra – originally launched by Pfizer to treat erectile dysfunction among mature men, is now keenly sought by young males who wish to enhance their sexual performance.

In 2004 the *International Journal of Impotence Research* published a study suggesting that the use of anti-impotence drugs by young men had soared. The research found that usage among men aged from 18 to 45 had increased by 312 per cent, while among men aged from 46 to 55 usage had increased by 216 per cent ('Patterns of use of sildenafil among commercially insured adults in the United States, 1998–2002', Volume 16, Number 4, August 2004). The previous year, in a story gleefully related by the tabloids, six British schoolboys aged 12 and 13 ended up in hospital after popping Viagra pills during their lunch break.

The *International Journal* suggested that marketing might be to blame for Viagra's new status as a recreational drug. 'With a direct to consumer advertising campaign, sildenafil has brought the recognition and treatment of ED [erectile dysfunction] to the forefront of public awareness. Originally, sildenafil [advertising] in the US was targeted to older males (e.g. using Bob Dole as spokesperson, print ad featuring grey-haired male dancing with grey-haired female), but it has been increasingly marketed to younger consumers (e.g. baseball player Rafael Palmeiro as a spokesperson, sponsoring Earth, Wind, and Fire concert tour).'

Whether Earth, Wind and Fire appeal to younger consumers is a moot point – but Viagra has also sponsored NASCAR in the form of a speeding blue automobile. In Brazil, ads for Viagra featuring local soccer legend Pele were taken off the air in 2005 when the government became 'alarmed at an increase in illicit use of anti-impotence drugs by youths'. Health Minister Humberto Costa said the ban was imposed following reports that young people were abusing the drugs to improve their sex lives. '"The uncontrolled use of these medicines can cause health problems, such as heart attacks," Costa said. The ban didn't mention Viagra by name, but was clearly aimed at ending a prominent publicity campaign.... The smiling 62-year-old Pele tells his fellow Brazilians in the ads that he doesn't need Viagra, but would use it if he did' ('Ban on impotence drug shelves Brazil's Pele Viaga campaign', *USA Today*, 26 July 2003).

One Australian doctor pinned the blame not on Viagra advertising, but on the media in general. Brett McCann, a senior lecturer in sexology at Sydney University and the chief executive of Impotence Australia, said, 'What we hear in the media, and culturally in the Western world, is really about good sex. Shows like *Sex and the City* are all about good sex and how important it is to perform sexually...When you look at how highly prized good sex is, or how (the community says) men should perform, it actually reinforces a myth... When young men have good sexual functioning and then also use drugs in the belief they are enhancing (their performance), using drugs they don't need, it's a concern' ('Love is the drug', *The Age*, Melbourne, 8 February 2005).

Ironically, the *International Journal of Impotence Research* says there is little evidence that Viagra enhances sexual performance among men who do not have erectile problems in the first place – except, perhaps, for the placebo effect of minimizing anxiety.

DON'T JUST DO IT

We still need to be told to use condoms. After a peak in usage following the arrival of AIDS in the 1980s, irresponsibility has once again taken hold. In the UK, the Health Protection Agency reports that sexually transmitted infections (STIs) are, alarmingly, thriving. Between 1995 and 2004, the number of STI diagnoses at clinics more than doubled. Reported cases of chlamydia were up by 223 per cent, gonorrhoea by 111 per cent and syphilis – although still rare, at 2,254 cases in 2004 – by 1,499 per cent. This trend continued the following year. HIV infection deriving from heterosexual contact is also on the rise: the number of diagnoses in the UK increased from 2031 in 2000 to 4049 in 2005 ('A Complex Picture – HIV and Other Sexually Transmitted Infections in the United Kingdom, 2006', HPA). And then there are unwanted pregnancies.

In 2005, a spokesman from the Men's Health Forum said he believed that 'more men were likely to have more than one sexual partner at any one time, the number of sexual partners men have per year is increasing, the number of men paying for sex has gone up, as has the number of men who have had a sexual partner'. Men are more likely to indulge in risk-taking behaviour, the same report suggested. Young men tend to treat casual sex as a combination of rite of passage and recreation, assuming they'll devote themselves to a steady partner some time in the future. The Forum spokesman described their sex lives as 'chaotic', with decisions often made 'under the influence of alcohol or drugs'. The problem of STIs is exacerbated by the fact that, as usual, men are reluctant to go to doctors and get themselves checked out – even if they're worried that they've caught something. 'Embarrassment is probably the single biggest reason why so few men visit genitourinary medicine clinics' ('Living very dangerously: men's sexual game of risk', *The Observer*, 27 November 2005).

Government agencies and the makers of condoms are trying hard to persuade consumers to practise safe sex. In the United States, apparently, they are not always helped by the media. The magazine *Advertising Age* reported that broadcasters seemed uncomfortable with condom advertising, despite a rise in the sexual content of programming. In September 2007, an organization called the Parents' Television Council claimed that sexual references had swelled by 22 per cent during early prime time compared with the same period six years earlier. And a 2005 study by the Kaiser Family Foundation said the number of sexual scenes on TV had almost doubled since 1998 ('Sex on TV is OK as long as it's not safe', 17 September 2007).

Yet both CBS and Fox rejected an ad for Trojan condoms. The spot showed women in a cocktail bar rejecting the advances of pigs in suits. When one of the pigs bought a packet of condoms from the vending machine in the bathroom, it morphed into a good-looking man. Fox said rejected the spot because 'contraceptive advertising must stress health-related uses rather than the prevention of pregnancy'.

This provides a hint of the social, political and religious sensi-tivities confronting condom manufacturers in the US. Product placement of condoms in TV shows with high sexual content is virtually non-existent. Jim Daniels, vice-president, marketing for Church & Dwight, Trojan's parent company, told *Ad Age* that he was 'frustrated' by broadcasters' attitudes. 'Sixty-five million Americans have an incurable STD. Three million unwanted pregnancies a year – half of which end in abortion... And yet you can advertise Viagra all you like, and Valtrex for [genital] herpes, but not advertise the condoms that would go on the erections and prevent herpes.'

The situation appears to be somewhat healthier in the United Kingdom. Ruth Gresty, marketing director of leading brand Durex, has successfully placed advertising 'on all commercial channels' over the past few years. The spots have promoted not just standard condoms, but also a model with a vibrating penis ring, as well as the company's brand of lubricant, Play. 'Condom advertising is featured after 9pm, and lubricant advertising after 11pm,' Gresty says.

One of the most successful Durex TV spots featured a young man being pursued through night-time city streets by hundreds of other men dressed as giant sperm. When he met and embraced his girlfriend, the sperm rushed forward to pounce on the couple – but were stopped short by an invisible wall of latex. The man and woman walked away in perfect safety, leaving the sperm to shove in vain against the impenetrable barrier. 'For a hundred million reasons', deadpanned the endline. Ironically, cheeky ads like this 2002 spot work well as 'viral' campaigns, spreading across the web like wildfire as the links are passed on from one user to the next.

'We've done print advertising in men's and women's magazines,' says Gresty. 'And advertising on the Underground is effective because public transport is used by many young professionals.'

To diffuse its message as widely as possible, Durex works closely with the government's health department, as well as organizations like (AIDS and HIV charity) the Terrence Higgins Trust, and media brands that appeal to young people, such as BBC Radio One and MTV. It has a close relationship with the DJ Tim Westwood, who has toured universities exhorting students to practise safe sex ('Strap it up before you slap it up!') while packing them onto dance floors. 'One of our strategies is to go to young people directly,' Gresty explains. 'So we give away condoms at universities, rock festivals and airports. There are obvious places where young people feel uninhibited and free to have sex – on holiday is one of them.'

Giving condoms away is one thing – ensuring wide availability the rest of the time is another. Durex encourages the installation of vending machines in bars and nightclubs and strives to make certain that these are fully stocked and well maintained. There are currently 35,000 of them in the United Kingdom. It also monitors the layout of pharmacies and supermarkets to ascertain that condoms can be purchased without effort.

'There's still an embarrassment factor to buying condoms, so we want them to be highly visible. Ideally they'd be next to the razor blades or the deodorant. Young men don't want to have to ask where the condoms are. As a brand, we see ourselves as a helper and a protector. We want to be there when you need us. That's why you'll see us everywhere from pubs to garage forecourts. To put it bluntly, if a man thinks he's pulled, he should be able to get his hands on a condom with minimum effort.'

Marketing activity seems biased towards young people – but what about older men? 'We reach men in their late twenties and thirties with ads in magazines like *Maxim* and *Men's Health*,' reassures Gresty. But she admits that there is a new generation of men that has barely been targeted with condom advertising at all.

'These are the empty-nesters – men who have just gone through a divorce and are now dating again. They've probably had the same partner for many years. They haven't used a condom for a long time, if ever. And if their new partner is a mature woman, they might assume that as there's no risk of unwanted pregnancy, they need not use a condom. But in fact there's been quite a dramatic rise in the incidence of STIs among older men. This is something we need to address.'

The phenomenon returns to one of the unifying themes of this book. Certain aspects of masculinity remain unaltered, hard-wired into our genes. But many facets of our lives have changed beyond recognition – including our most intimate relationships.

BRANDING TOOLKIT

- The internet has made the dating game easier for men.

- Men are assailed by sexual imagery in media and advertising.

- Very little of this is advertising promoting safe sex.

- The landscape of sexual relationships has dramatically changed.

- Men are staying single for longer and getting divorced earlier.

- More men indulge in risk-taking sexual behaviour than ever before.

Conclusion

Men 2.0

Male consumers still exist. Although some marketers insist that gender is irrelevant, others confirm that men respond to marketing messages in unique and specific ways. No matter how much society has changed, it goes against common sense and our own personal experiences to suggest that male and female consumers are becoming as one. If that were the case, the marketers of cars wouldn't be so terrified of giving their vehicles feminine traits.

The idea of gender neutrality is perhaps more relevant in the context of younger consumers. Young men are as different from their elders as they ever were – but they would look utterly alien to previous generations. Today's young Western male is more likely to experiment with the signifiers of gender, and even with his own sexuality. Certainly, he is far more likely to have gay friends and to share certain attitudes and preferences with them. But this is not a book about marketing to teenagers – and it seems to me that the consumption habits of men become more interesting when they reach their mid twenties. During that time, they are busy constructing their adult identities, bolting on various brands that they will be reluctant to change in the years to come.

Happily for marketers, the brands that men prefer display certain collective attributes. Functionality comes through time and time again – men will buy into science, technology or engineering. It's almost as though they yearn to strengthen and improve their own physical capabilities (this may also explain their love of gadgets). They care more about aesthetics than they would like to admit, but mere surface flash is not enough. They look for the telling detail that shows them that the designer of this object – be it a shirt, a shaver, or a seat on a plane – has understood their needs, and gone the extra mile to satisfy them.

Authenticity is another thread. Men are so baffled by the choices available to them that they seek a concrete reason to trust a brand. Resisters by nature, they are not entirely happy that craftsmanship has been replaced by 'Made in China'. They do not want to be taken in by another bottle of gunk, another badly-made jacket. And so they look for longevity, heritage and craftsmanship. If none of these are available, familiarity will do.

Men are loyal consumers – and brands should be careful not to offend them. They like to be treated with deference and respect. The corporate travel industry has grasped this very well. Health clubs are getting there. The retailers of men's clothing – apart from a handful of tailors and luxury brands – still have a long way to go.

It's worth remembering that a lot of men are preoccupied by status. No doubt due to their natural competitiveness, they like to use brands to show off. Whether it's an item of clothing, a car, a mobile phone, a watch or a newspaper, men find satisfaction in the symbols of success.

And yet they feel the need to be discreet. They like everything they do to look effortless, without fuss. The concept of 'cool' – of maintaining a composed, aloof distance – is essentially masculine. That's why the new men's spas resemble the gentlemen's clubs of old – everything goes on behind closed doors. It's also why men like buying stuff online: what better way of looking as though you don't care about shopping than to make purchases from your desk? Internet retail for men is a highly promising area.

By the way, it is absurd to think that men do not care about their appearance. They care in greater or lesser degrees – but many of them care a great deal. It's only for the last hundred years or so that men have been obliged to choose from a restricted range of clothing – the suit and the coat, the T-shirt and the jeans. At earlier moments in history, men favoured adornment. They wore powdered wigs and lace, jackets heavy with brocade and pearls. Even Beau Brummell, who spearheaded the shift towards pared-down dressing, would spend hours fiddling with a necktie. That was all about status, too. The obsession with designer sports shoes among some young men is just a modern expression of the same urge. Our rediscovery of style and grooming is not an aberration, but a return to form.

We just need it to look effortless, that's all. Men love it when the woman in their life tells them they look great – but they hate it when she turns to her friend and adds, 'Of course, he spends longer in the bathroom than I do.' Perhaps one day, this kind of remark will have faded back into history. Either way, I have the feeling that metrosexuality is here to stay.

All of this makes men sound rather pompous and unapproachable – a bit up themselves. But in fact, men are rather good at relaxing. They socialize easily, especially with one another. They enjoy humour, and marketing messages that incorporate a touch of it go down well with them. They are more creative than they are given credit for. Men are artists and chefs as well as soldiers and builders. They are musicians, too. In fact music is an important part of their lives – particularly for those under 40. They don't read many novels, it seems – but they're addicted to newspapers, especially the sports pages. Oh yes, the stereotype is accurate – they adore sport. According to ESPN, 94 per cent of American men aged 18 to 34 consider themselves sports fans.

On the face of it, men sound like a pretty straightforward bunch. But wait a minute – aren't they supposed to be confused? Aren't they struggling to redefine their role in a gender-neutral society? There's no arguing with the fact that men's status has changed. It seems a long time since the Western male was able to put his feet up, smug and unchallenged in his role of protector and provider, while the little woman vacuumed around him. Society may not be entirely equal – men still earn more than women – but we know that it has come a long way.

My feeling, though, is that men are achieving equilibrium. They have realized that they can't change certain immutable aspects of their nature: their pragmatism, their aggressiveness, their need to compete. But having scurried off in search of their feminine sides, then rushed back to defend the citadel of manhood, they are slowly realizing that they might be able to have it all. Why shouldn't they wear great clothes, look after their health, pay attention to their appearance, have a family life and hold down a high-powered job? Why shouldn't they be bluff and practical, but also sensitive and vulnerable? Why shouldn't they, in short, be Men 2.0?

This might sound like an idle fantasy, or an attempt to stick yet another label on male consumers. Honestly, I think that's the last thing we need. But when I look around – at my friends, at the people I've met or interviewed for this book – I see a lot of positive, well-balanced men. None of them seem to be harbouring a complex about their threatened masculinity. Some of them are living alone, enjoying the last few years of independence before they settle down. Others are married to talented and hard-working women. And a lot of these men, despite rumours to the contrary, having nothing against shopping. But they remain elusive and demanding; traits that have, for many brands, made them the ultimate target group.

References

BOOKS

Anderson, Arnold, Cohn, Leigh and Holbrook, Thomas (2000), *Making Weight: Men's Conflicts with Food, Shape and Appearance*, Gürze Books, Carlsbad, California

Antongiavanni, Nicholas (2006), *The Suit*, HarperCollins, New York

Breward, Christopher (1999), *The Hidden Consumer: Masculinities, Fashion and City Life 1860–1914*, Manchester University Press, Manchester

Butterfield, Leslie (2005), *Enduring Passion: The Story of the Mercedes-Benz Brand*, John Wiley & Sons, Chichester

Elms, Robert (2005), *The Way We Wore*, Picador, London

Flusser, Alan (2002), *Dressing the Man: Mastering the Art of Permanent Fashion*, HarperCollins, New York

Foulkes, Nick (2005), *Dunhill by Design*, Flammarion, Paris

Kiley, David (2004), *Driven: Inside BMW, The Most Admired Car Company in the World*, John Wiley & Sons, Hoboken, New Jersey

Mansfield, Harvey C. (2006), *Manliness*, Yale University Press, New Haven, Connecticut and London

Salzman, Marian, Matatha, Ira and O'Reilly, Ann (2005), *The Future of Men*, Palgrave Macmillan, New York

Winder, Simon (2006), *The Man Who Saved Britain*, Picador, London

ONLINE RESOURCES

Ask Men (www.askmen.com)
Advertising Age (www.adage.com)
BBC News (www.news.bbc.co.uk)
Brandweek (www.brandweek.com)
Cosmetics Design Europe (www.cosmeticsdesign-europe.com)
Esomar (www.esomar.com)
Health Protection Agency (www.hpa.org.uk)
LexisNexis (www.lexisnexis.com)
Men's Health Forum (www.menshealthforum.org.uk)
Salon.com (www.salon.com)
Wired (www.wired.com)
World Advertising Research Centre (www.warc.com)
World Health Organization (www.who.int)
Worth Global Style Network (www.wgsn.com)

Index